Understanding and Dealing with Everyday Racism

THE SIX STAGES FRAMEWORK

Dr Shungu Hilda M'gadzah

MSc, BSc (Hons), PGCE, EdPsychDoc, CPsychol

Published by Swan & Horn 2022
Email: info@swanandhorn.co.uk

ISBN KDP paperback version 978-1-909675-31-5
ISBN Kindle version 978-1-909675-32-2

British Library Cataloguing in Publication Data: A catalogue record for this book is available from the British Library

Website: www.sixstagesframework.com
Email: contact@sixstagesframework.com
Telephone: +44 7956 965266

Cover image by Hassan Sahib (HasanKa)
Graphics by Shona M'gadzah, Sophie Hampshire and Maria Carter

Contents

Acknowledgements

Particular thanks go to all those who have contributed to my thinking in the area of diversity, equity and inclusion, especially those within my LinkedIn Network; to my friend and publisher Maria Carter for all her support; and to my daughter Shona – always the voice of reason (I am so proud of you).

Many thanks also to Sarah Lacey, Nicholas Cheffings, Colin Gordon, Penny Holding and Amanda Mwale for reading and commenting on my book prior to publication; and to Sally Casterton, Tatenda Mutsvairo and Kudzai (Donnie) Madziya, Hannah Jarrett for their support and encouragement.

Thanks also to Marie Odhiambo, Amber Johnson (and Jasmine Jordan) (Honorary Psychology Assistants) for supporting me with the design of the *Six Stages* assessments.

Particular thanks to my friend Giovanna Stevenson Ostacchini for all her work on designing the website and formulating the assessments.

Praise for this book

"Dr M'gadzah tackles head on the issues of modern-day racism. The book is set within the difficult, turbulent and often unsettling world of today. It inspires interest by referring to current affair issues such as the tragic death of George Floyd, the Black Lives Matter Movement and 'the Harry and Meghan' interview with Oprah Winfrey. By using popular cultural references, such as the books The Colour Purple (Alice Walker), Dr M'gadzah engages the reader wholeheartedly. The Six Stages Framework promotes optimism and empathy at a time of great need."

Sarah Lacey BA(Hons), PGCE, MA

"This is an excellent read and covers the key areas of diversity, equity and inclusion in a thorough and systematic manner. I would like to congratulate the author on her thoroughness. The contents of the book encourage learning organisations to be reflective through self-assessment. When taken seriously, action plans will be converted to actions, and positive differences will be seen and celebrated, from the individual level right up to the institutional level – no-one should be left out."

Dr Colin Gordon, Ex-Principal Educational Psychologist BSc, PGCE, MA, MSc, DocEdPsych, CPsychol, AFBPsS, SARSM

"I think this book is very clear. The examples you use from the media are really interesting and engaging, and most importantly very relevant in today's climate! I like how you included both the positive and negative axes and how racism or growth can progress in either direction. I really valued reading about non-white racism towards black people – this book sheds light on this issue that clearly also needs to be thought about much more. It was really insightful to read the author's thoughts on the development of shared empathy to open up conversations about race and difference. I also liked the ideas about solidarity and common humanity in bringing people together towards a common understanding. I think seeing each other's humanity is vitally important, because we are dealing with a history of the inhumane treatment of one group of people for the benefit of another. I appreciated reading about how we care for people of colour's mental health because of the toll it takes on us to have these conversations or even to witness the issues of racism ongoing in different ways. Great work!"

Dr Amanda Mwale, Clinical Psychologist CPsychol

Foreword

by Nicholas Cheffings

Past Global Chair of the international law firm Hogan Lovells, now focusing on advocacy for diversity, inclusion, anti-racism, equity and equality in business and society—August 2021

This is a book for our times. It is about diversity, racism and inclusion, but it is so much more than that. It is informed by the author's lived experiences and it draws heavily upon her training as a psychologist. It speaks of the challenges that our society faces and it explains how we can rise to those challenges.

This is not a book that leaves the reader dispirited or disillusioned, wondering how we found ourselves in this mess and despairing over whether things will ever really change. It explores the 'caves of privilege' that are so prevalent in our society. It encourages us all to come out of those caves and to build 'bridges of empathy'. But – critically – it does not leave us wondering how on earth we are meant to get from 'cave to bridge'. It guides us along the path, recognising that we might occasionally lose our footing.

Dr Shungu Hilda M'gadzah's thoughtful *Six Stages Framework* recognises the definitions of racism, and it also shows us that we need to expand our thinking around racism if we are to achieve *real change*. While illustrating her observations with recent examples of discrimination against racial minorities, and of anti-blackness in particular, the author recognises that biases and prejudice exist in all racial groups. She encourages us all to evaluate our biases and to make the space for honest conversations without judgement.

The message in this book is very clear. We cannot, and must not, carry on as we are. We have to put an end to empty posturing. We have to stop polarising issues of race and going to extremes when we talk about racial equity, inclusion and racism. We are shown how, put simply, we have a *shared* responsibility to try to understand each other's values, beliefs, perceptions and realities. It is only by beginning such conversations that the possibility of change exists.

This book helps us not simply to understand what we need to do, but also how we can go and do it. It provides a toolkit for individuals, governments, schools, universities and businesses. It takes us, with clear examples and explanations, on the journey – wherever we may start that journey – to a place where we are all able to take on leadership roles in promoting racial equity, inclusion and social justice. It shows us how we can join together with others to challenge social injustice and racism – to do so for the sake of humanity. It is predicated on the unarguable proposition that there is far more that unites us than there is that separates us. This is a book that is firmly rooted in our uncomfortable reality, yet is optimistic about our future. It shows us that, by following the *Six Stages Framework*, we really can make the world a better place.

Introduction

At the heart of the *Six Stages Framework* is a psychological tool that is designed to assess where individual people and whole organisations are in their journey towards understanding and dealing with the issues surrounding racial equity,[1] inclusion and racism.

The purpose of this book is to describe the Six Stages conceptual framework for understanding and dealing with racism.

The Framework recognises the importance of tackling broader issues pertaining to diversity and inclusion – not just in the area of racial equity and diversity, but also related to other areas such as cultural, gender, disability and sexual orientation. It explores the importance of understanding issues of identity and intersectionality and the key barriers that exist in terms of inclusion.

This book describes the ideas, key concepts and principles underpinning the Six Stages Framework. It explains why this approach is important for such a sensitive issue and outlines the range of courses, training and coaching provided. Inclusion Psychologists Ltd offer bespoke coaching, mentoring, consultancy and training programmes on these issues to both individuals and organisations across all sectors. Assessments are available for individuals, schools, universities, local authorities, businesses and boards, and for other organisations including charities.

The assessments help to establish a baseline position that can be used to measure progress and outcomes. They can be used along with other sources of information and data in a triangulated approach. We also offer diversity, equity and inclusion (DEI) courses, coaching and supervision to individuals, groups, DEI consultants and other professional groups such as educational psychologists. The efficacy of the framework as a tool for change and transformation, one which can be used by organisations and individuals to provide support and challenge in this area, is explored.

[1] Equality means each individual or group of people is given the same resources or opportunities. Equity recognises that each person has different circumstances and allocates the exact resources and opportunities needed to reach an equal outcome (Gutoskey, 2020).

List of figures and tables

Figures

Tables

1

Tackling racism using the *Six Stages Framework*

The *Six Stages Framework* is a psychological tool that is designed to assess where individual people or organisations are in their journey towards understanding and dealing with the complexities of individual and systemic racism, whether that is conscious or unconscious, overt or covert, direct or indirect (Equality Act, 2010).

Central to the framework is the understanding that we are all at different stages of a journey towards our ability to deal with racism and to creating a more equitable and inclusive society. An individual person or organisation can be at different stages of a journey in terms of their ability to foster inclusion for diverse groups. The framework can easily be adapted and applied to other areas of diversity and used to chart individual's and organisation's journeys in these areas.

The key to promoting change is understanding the overriding reasons and the story of where each individual is on that journey as well as in providing a safe space where they can be supported to develop and challenge themselves so that they can relate more effectively with those who are different.

Embracing diversity and inclusion work and anti-racism training should not be about conflict. The key ingredients for the support and challenge we offer are compassion, empathy and understanding without blame or judgement.

The *Six Stages* is a conceptual framework that uses a dynamic model and a number of developmental matrices to address the most pertinent aspects of the challenges that we all face today. Current values, attitudes and perceptions relating to racial equity and inclusion are assessed within the framework, and bespoke training can be provided that enhances an understanding about differences, and in particular racism.

The framework and training help to identify personal and organisational beliefs, attitudes and behaviours, and reformulate these by challenging perceptions and prejudices. Each stage of the framework includes the required support for exploring racism in social, political, educational institutions and workplace arenas.

The specialist bespoke developmental programme and support is essential because this is such a sensitive issue. There are seven different types of diversity assessments, each tailored for different groups and sectors. These are:

- individuals
- organisations
- boards and governing bodies
- infant children (ages 3–5)
- primary school pupils (ages 6–11)
- secondary school pupils (ages 11–18)
- university students.

2

What is the purpose of the *Six Stages Framework*?

In short, the *Six Stages Framework* contributes to creating a safe and more equitable society, one that is free of discrimination, and specifically racial inequity and injustice. It does so by supporting individuals and organisations to play their part in dealing with these issues. Work in this area has never been more urgent. Racism and intolerance impact on society as a whole, and fear, anger and blame feed the monster. The case will be made that diversity and inclusion relates to and impacts on every single person, regardless of their race, colour, age, gender, sexual orientation, status, and physical or mental health. For this reason, racial equity and inclusion needs to become everybody's business, not just an issue for black and ethnic minority (BEM)[2] groups.

The framework reminds us that we are humans first and that we have so much in common to unite us. Above all, it reminds us of the overwhelming benefits of diversity and inclusion. This work calls for individuals to act as ripples of change, requiring us to be aware, sensitive, mindful and curious as well as empathetic, compassionate and brave. We have to understand and recognise our differences and be able to talk about them. We must also be able to challenge prejudice, discrimination and racism wherever we see it, whether that be in the home, community, school, university or workplace. We need to open up and own up to our biases, actively working to combat them in order to be better citizens in an increasingly diverse world.

As Prince Harry said during his interview with Oprah Winfrey in March 2021, we all need to "do the work and to do our own learning" when it comes to racism. The *Six Stages Framework* supports us with this task.

These have been difficult and traumatic years

The year 2020 will be remembered by many as a traumatic year for a number of reasons. As the world was brought to its knees by the Covid-19 pandemic, many issues of racial injustice were thrown into the spotlight. In the USA on 25 May, a police officer pushed

2 The author recognises the problem with this generic term; this will be discussed in the subsequent pages.

his knee down onto a black man's neck for eight minutes and 46 seconds and watched him die. His murder was watched by millions of people worldwide in total disbelief. Thousands of outraged people around the world took to the streets in solidarity to protest and demand '*Never again!*'.

George Floyd was the name of the man who was killed, and his death sparked worldwide protests and condemnation. Many questioned how something like this could happen in broad daylight with such an apparent disregard for the value of a person's life, simply because they had a different skin colour – disregard for the life of a black man.

Later, in January 2021, right-wing extremists invaded the US Capitol building in Washington demanding that the USA election outcome, which saw Joe Biden of the Democratic Party win a majority over Republican candidate and former-US president, Donald Trump, be overturned. People around the world were understandably shaken by this attack. Far-reaching discussions followed on how worried society should be about what is at stake, and many concluded that it is our democratic way of life and liberal values.

For many, the dangers posed by right-wing extremists are clear—they define the world in a certain way and are outraged when others don't agree with them. Comments like these (heard on a CNN News broadcast) were commonplace:

> *They want to deny everyone else their rights and those at the most risk are the marginalized groups and ethnic minorities.*

For many, there were concerns that society is nurturing individuals who are intolerant of differences, and that ordinary families are being radicalised by extremist groups who, because of the colour of their skin, feel entitled and will 'stop at nothing to snatch power away from others'. Surprisingly, none of the protesters were arrested during the storming of the Capitol – in stark contrast to the earlier George Floyd protests.

Both of these incidents highlight what happens when anger, blame, intolerance and prejudice are left unchecked and the need for change in the area of racial inequity and racism is continually ignored and dismissed. Some people try to argue that the above incidents are an American issue – that they wouldn't happen in their own back yards!

Matt Hancock, the UK Health Secretary, said on the BBC News (2020):

> *Thankfully, this is all based in response to events in America rather than here, but we also must continue the drive here for tolerance and genuine equality of opportunity.*

The truth, however, is that these things can happen, and they do. They happen anywhere a sense of power, privilege and entitlement remains unchallenged, and where there is intolerance of differences and eagerness to lay blame on those who do not resemble us, including ethnic minorities.

Make no mistake, this issue applies to us all. However, it sometimes seems that some of us exist within 'caves of privilege' (Woodward, 2020) and feel sheltered from the injustices that affect marginalised groups. This can lead us to believe that matters of racial equity and inclusion are not our business. However, such attitudes nurture and reinforce messages of superiority, entitlement and intolerance. The impact of this kind of selective perspective cannot be underestimated.

Prejudice, racism and fear of differences

It is indisputable that certain groups within society face the negative consequences of bias (Agarwal, 2020). Each of us assumes a different role and position in society, defined and influenced by our individual characteristics such as gender, sexuality, racial and cultural background, and physical and mental health. People are often divided and placed into different categories according to these factors, and social constructs, like race, impose hierarchies of power and negative attitudes that serve to limit the outcomes of certain groups. The combined forces of prejudice, racism and hierarchies of power creates systems that discriminate – systems in which there is no space for diversity, equity or inclusion.

Afua Hirsch, author of the 2018 book *Brit(ish): On Race, Identity and Belonging*, speaks openly about her experiences of racism, of being made to feel unwelcome as a black person, and how this made her reflect on her identity. Discussing the ways she has been treated, she states:

> *That told me there was something taboo, problematic and unwelcome about my identity. ... It was as if the way I looked required a longer explanation. There weren't many other people around here who looked like me and I faced a constant struggle trying to pretend my otherness didn't exist, attempting to fit in. I spent my whole life wondering is this really my country, is this truly where I belong?*

Clearly there was nothing problematic about her identity; it's more that she began to feel there was something problematic based on how she was being treated.

The attitudes and behaviours of individuals and organisations are informed by their experiences and those around them. Our values and belief systems are influenced by our peers, parents and the society in which we live in, and the messages and information we are exposed to. Unfortunately, many of us find ourselves within communities or systems that view and define us through the lens of stereotype and discrimination, making it difficult for us to thrive and achieve our potential or – worse still – pose a threat to our mental health. For these negative experiences to change, everyone in society must take responsibility for the change that is required. We must support individuals and organisations to re-evaluate their values, beliefs, attitudes and behaviours. In doing so, we – as a society – can embrace differences, diversity and inclusion, and create a sense of community and spaces in which we all feel safe and experience a sense of belonging .

For this to happen, we need to be able to question and re-examine some of the things we've been taught (or not taught) as children about those who are different, including different cultural and racial groups. To achieve this, we have to start having honest conversations about racial differences and how racism manifests itself. We need to stop seeing these topics as taboo and stop hoping that if we remain silent and turn the other way the issues will go away – they will not.

Values, attitudes and beliefs

Racism is a problem faced by all of us; tackling it is not just down to those who are white and privileged. Yasmin Alibhai-Brown (2020) spoke about South Asian prejudice and Asian anti-black racism in an article entitled 'Racism is not just a white problem – It's time we Asians confronted our own prejudices'. When describing the prejudice and racism directed at black people, she explained:

> *Too many second-generation Asians unquestioningly tolerate these (racist) values, like one 'lovely' Asian pair whom Darshna and Chi befriended on holiday. The couple invited them over for a weekend but could not accommodate them because his mother would not have a black man in the family home. Many Asians have never acknowledged or confronted this ingrained racism ... When Nimmi tries to interrogate the belief systems and mindsets, she faces pushback, dismay and fury. She keeps on going, battling against 'backward views which have no place in the 21st century. What about empathy and shared humanity? Why do Asians still want to marry fair-skinned people? It is a way to maintain prestige and position. Call it 'light privilege'.*

Unfortunately some of our belief systems and some of the things we've been taught are not grounded in fact. Instead, they are based on stereotypes and fear of differences and the unknown. Often, these are irrational fears that perpetuate and keep us separate from those who are different, especially different racial groups. Some might say they are innate responses or the result of evolutionary programming or learned thinking (Agarwal, 2020) – no longer fit for purpose.

Whatever the origins, they serve to preserve the sense of entitlement and that supposedly keeps us safe and secure within our 'caves of privilege' (Woodward, 2020). Maintaining such positions can be limiting for individuals and organisations because they do not promote inclusion or diversity of thought, which are key to effective business success and performance (Hock, 2019; Syed, 2020).

To break free from so-called caves, we need to continually explore and challenge ourselves, those around us and the organisations we work within. We need to be able to question and challenge the belief systems that serve to discriminate against and stop the advancement of those who are different, whatever those differences might be. The *Six Stages Framework* supports people as they begin to face these challenges, starting with recognising inequity and differential treatment in all its forms, finding ways of talking about it and putting in place solutions to counter it.

Calls for wider cultural changes in society—women are angry at the perceived lack of focus on their safety

Following the abduction and murder of Sarah Everard in March 2021 by a London Metropolitan Police officer, concerns have been raised about the safety of women on the streets, and there are calls for women to 'reclaim the streets'. Women continue to actively protest against harassment and violence against them, and calling for laws that will make misogyny a hate crime. People are saying 'It's time to educate your sons'.

While abductions and murders of women are rare, thankfully, there exists a spectrum that has harassment at one end and extreme violence, abduction and murder at the other. Thousands of women are coming together to share their experiences and have complained about harassment from men on the streets, at home, in nightclubs, on public transport, and at work.

Similarly, it can be argued that there is a spectrum of racism, with prejudice at one end and extreme racism, including violence and murder, at the other (Fig. 6 on pages 92-93). Furthermore, within the area of DEI, other spectra can be produced that relate to gender, or disability or LGBTQ+ bias and discrimination, showing the progression of beliefs, attitudes and behaviours from low levels to extreme levels. It should be possible to design assessments that identify where individuals and organisations are in relation to each of these DEI areas and to use these as tools for assessments and conversations as tools for change.

The murder of Sarah Everard has left women (and parents) feeling anxious and angry, crying out that enough is enough! A vigil held in South London in Sarah Everard's honour saw hundreds of women turn out to share their grief. Despite the police presence, the Duchess of Cambridge went out in support of the protesters and laid flowers in her memory. She stated in an interview:

> *I know what it feels like to feel unsafe walking on the streets before I was married.*

When I heard this, I couldn't help but wonder whether this quote might unintentionally reinforce some of the misogyny I am talking about. I say this because a colleague commented, "It is like the Duchess is saying she was really vulnerable on the streets before she married a man (prince) to protect her".

Still, her response is an example of empathy in action – empathy for Sarah Everard and for other people who are outraged by the incident. This sense of grief, loss and anger was shared by black people all across the world, including the USA; they stood in solidarity during the George Floyd protests because they understand how it feels to be unsafe at the hands of the police. This flow of empathy was seen in people who are not black; similarly, in the case of Sarah Everard, many men joined in with protests about violence against women. Unfortunately, the police response to Sarah Everard's vigil (and to the George Floyd protests) was open to criticism because of their behaviour. In the former there were concerns about the manhandling of women by men. However, some noticed that times are changing, like Scottish actress Kelly Macdonald. In March 2021 she said:

> *The world is a different place to how it used to be a year ago and it's making everybody think about life differently and how to live it well and people are having these important conversations – such as the Me-Too movement and women's safety.*

Across the world, there are calls for cultural change relating to racial intolerance, injustice, women's safety and general inequity. The attitudes and behaviours that were tolerated in the past are no longer now acceptable. The *Six Stages Framework* helps us reflect on cultural changes within society, to initiate difficult conversations about differences, attitudes and behaviours, and to explore their impact on those who are different.

Athletes and sportspeople protest against racial injustice

Worldwide, this group of society has begun protesting against social injustice, racism and police brutality. In the USA athletes began 'taking the knee' during the US national anthem, back in August 2016. This has become a sign of silent solidarity, demonstrating support for human rights during times of political turmoil (Sinnott, 2021; Siregar, 2020).

At a press conference in September 2016, Colin Kaepernick (an American civil rights activist and former football quarterback) openly expressed his opinions on the matter after 'sitting out' during the national anthem. His words were reported by Woodward and Mindock (2020):

> *I am not going to stand up to show pride in a flag for a country that oppresses black people and people of colour ... To me, this is bigger than football, and it would be selfish on my part to look the other way. There are bodies in the street and people getting paid leave and getting away with murder.*

He protested against police brutality towards African–Americans and institutional racism. He has not been signed to another league since. Some players took the knee to show their opposition to Donald Trump. Their actions divided nations. Some refer to them as unpatriotic and disrespectful, believing that social issues have no place in the sporting world. Others view them as being patriotic and politically motivated, and praised them for being socially aware and taking a stand against social injustice.

Two weeks after the killing of George Floyd in June 2021, Roger Goodell, the National Football League (NFL) commissioner, issued an apology following years of debate within the NFL among fans and people criticising the footballers. Megan Rapinoe, star of the US national team, was the first soccer player to 'silently protest against racial inequality and follow in the footsteps of Kaepernick'. She took to the knee during the national anthem in the September 2016 NWSL match between the Chicago Red Stars and Seattle Reign (Siregar, 2020).

She stated that:

> *Being a gay American, I know what it means to look at the flag and not have it protect all of your liberties.*

Debates continue on the subject of taking the knee and how, according to some, it transcends sport as an extreme political act. It has become a serious talking point in international football. The way the media handles 'taking the knee' is highly relevant to how we embrace issues of racial justice. It can also be used to understand the 'six stages' described in this book, depending on the perspective taken by journalists and readers.

In June 2021, English footballer Raheem Sterling was awarded an MBE in the Queen's Birthday Honours list for outstanding achievement, specifically for his work on tackling racial inequality and racism in football. He has received many other awards (e.g. the Integrity and Impact Award at the BT Sport Industry Awards), but this one seems to be exceptional – both political and pivotal – in the current climate.

The pandemic heralds the way for greater understanding, compassion and empathy for those who are suffering

Covid-19 has brought untold suffering and uncertainty into our lives. In a recent post on LinkedIn, I found myself reflecting on an Instagram live interview by Nina Simonds, Leadership Facilitator and Executive Coach (2021) I had watched, about coping with chronic illness and the leadership lessons that arise from this.

I also reflected on a conversation I'd had with Jane Green, Educationalist lead for the new School Toolkit for Ehlers–Danlos syndrome and hypermobility disorders for UK schools; she is also an advocate for autism and neurodiverse hypermobility, as well as a speaker, and the Chair and Founder of SEDS (Sussex Ehlers–Danlos syndrome group).

I reflected on the challenges and lockdown anxieties many were faced with on a daily basis and how the pandemic further compounded these challenges on top of their existing pain and suffering. These conversations highlight the learning which exists in any challenge and how it can be generalised to other areas of life. Simonds explored the leadership lessons Rebecca Scott had learned from dealing with multiple sclerosis and "how they apply to leading through any complex challenge".

I wrote (M'gadzah, 2021):

> *I can't help but think that the pandemic has brought a new understanding and appreciation for those suffering from silent disabilities and the unacknowledged suffering of so many, when you go through a chronic illness and having to navigate this. We now have an insight and preview into some of the suffering many endure including children. It has brought new-found compassion and empathy as we all*

> *come to terms with feelings of helplessness and dealing with uncertainty, requiring us to hold onto what we are grateful for and how to build resilience and new hope.*

I believe it is important to view diversity, equity and inclusion in the same way and identify learning points (across different areas of inequity) and ask how these can be generalised to other areas of inequity. Queen Rania of Jordan was interviewed in February 2021 on CNN News, where she highlighted the importance of human relations and the need for more compassion:

> *One of the lessons that this pandemic has reinforced is that human relations are the cornerstones in our lives. When things are tough, we rely on each other to get through, and that applies to our globalized world. This crisis has shone a light on our common humanity and vulnerability but also exasperated and exacerbated the differences and divisions amongst us. So for the millions of people already struggling in poor countries, the old normal was a nightmare and we know that women, low-wage workers and minority groups everywhere have been impacted disproportionately. So I think the new normal needs to be more inclusive and equitable; it has to be more resilient and sustainable. It really has to be more compassionate.*

We have also seen many people, including sports personalities, talking about their mental health. Naomi Osaka, professional tennis player, reflected on the intense media scrutiny she has had to endure. In *Time Magazine*, 2021, she stated:

> *Issues that are so obvious to me at face value, like wearing a mask in a pandemic or kneeling to show support for anti-racism, are ferociously contested.*

Osaka also wrote about why 'It's okay to not be okay', and the need to prioritise her mental health (Osaka, 2021). On the CNN News, she spoke about her experience of depression and anxiety. Joshua Adams (2021) reflected on her words in *Time Magazine*, stating that:

> *Osaka also lamented that as a professional athlete, people treat her mental health needs sceptically. She recounted the great amount of pressure to disclose my symptoms – frankly because the press and the tournament did not believe me. Osaka implored readers to remember that athletes are human and needing to disclose the details of their mental health issues is something most people don't have to do in the workplace.*

Many have concluded that the tennis community needs to make changes to preserve players' mental health. There certainly seems to be a theme of failure by the media and others to see certain groups and individuals as human beings and an inability to show empathy for their experiences and suffering. Simone Biles, an American artistic gymnast, withdrew from the 2021 Olympic finals on vault, uneven bars and floor exercise, stating that she had to protect her mental health. Later, in an interview, she said:

> *It wasn't easy pulling out of all those competitions. People just thought it was easy, but I physically and mentally was not in the right head space, and I didn't want to jeopardize my health and my safety because, at the end of the day, it's not worth it.*

Biles explained that she had experienced "a little bit of the twisties" in the lead up to the events and felt unsafe, no longer trusting her ability to compete. She wondered what was happening to her – in her words: "Where did the wires not connect?".

How scary it must be to be in the middle of a routine, high in the air, and be unable to trust your body or rely on your perceptions and judgement. She spoke of the effects of this on her mental health and reminded us that sportspeople are not just there for our entertainment:

> *My mental and physical health is above all medals that I could ever win ... We're not just entertainment, we're humans ... And there are things going on behind the scenes that we're also trying to juggle with as well on top of sports.*

Biles' words echoed those of Osaka and within their comments is a plea to us all to treat them with compassion and empathy – not just as figures of spectacle. If we are to have true diversity and inclusion in society, including in the worlds of sport and work, we need to listen to the words and experiences of those who are brave enough to speak up about their experiences and what they are having to endure. Often, we will never know the suffering that goes on for many (whether it involves chronic illness, mental health or DEI issues) unless we are prepared to listen and truly empathise, and then we must show compassion.

The *Six Stages Framework* is a challenge and a call to all of us to show greater compassion and understanding, not just to those who are the same as us or whose experiences we relate to, but to all human beings.

Caves of privilege—recognising our privilege and sense of entitlement

In an interview between Bob Woodward and the then-president of the USA, Donald Trump, in June 2020, Woodward proposed a question to Trump about privilege:

> *We share one thing in common, we are white and privileged; my father was a lawyer and a judge in Illinois and we know what your father did ... Do you have any sense that privilege has isolated and put you in a cave to some extent, as it put me – and I think a lot of white privileged people are in a cave – in that we have to work our way out to understand the anger and the pain, particularly for black people in this country?*

Donald Trump replied:

> *No. You really drunk the Kool-Aid, didn't you? Wow! Listen to you. I don't feel that at all!*

It was clear from this interview that Woodward was able to empathise with the experiences of black people in ways that Trump did not. After listening to this interview, I introduced the concept of 'coming out of caves of privilege' into the *Six Stages Framework* (M'gadzah, 2020), as it resonates with many of the ideas in the framework. We each need to recognise the different caves of privilege we inhabit and consider how they have been constructed. We need to ask ourselves: *How deep inside my cave of privilege am I?*

These caves are constructed through our values, beliefs and cultural influences, and our sense of entitlement. From a young age, we receive different messages from our environment that help us construct our caves; for some of us, we continue going into our caves, deeper and deeper, holding on to what we have learnt, what we have seen and what we have been told, despite any evidence or facts. Some people inhabit caves of privilege related to gender and misogyny; for others it's race and discrimination. However, some caves are not of our own making and we find ourselves inhabiting them without being actively misogynistic or racist.

One day, we may find ourselves deep within a cave, having furnished it with tables, chairs and beds, and living there, seemingly secure from the outside world and unaware of the realities facing others. After some time, it can become difficult to understand or empathise with the experiences of others. We may struggle to show compassion just because they are different from us, as though our internal empathy and compassion switches have been turned off; as if we inhabit different worlds seen through a lens of safety from our cave.

The truth is that all of us have biases and prejudices, and for some of us, it is easier to lean towards the familiar, what we are used to, than to lead towards the unknown. We all have our own self-made caves, constructed in different ways according to our specific experiences, the contexts in which we have lived and grown, and the biases, stereotypes and prejudices we harbour or have been exposed to. Such biases and prejudices are often seen in the workplace where discrimination can occur towards those who are different when adaptations or flexible working arrangements are needed for some reason.

In addition, we all experience 'negative automatic thoughts' (Hollon and Kendall, 1980) that constantly pop into our heads as we observe and judge others, serving to reinforce and perpetuate our prejudices and the existence (and renovations!) of our caves.

It is important for us to acknowledge that we all have negative thoughts about others, and recognise how they are often amplified when we interact with those who differ from us or who do not fit into the boxes we have created.

It is also important to remember that it is perfectly natural to have these thoughts – however, we must challenge and correct them if we are to create truly inclusive environments.

When we look for things that reinforce our negative beliefs and keep us apart from those who are different, we take ourselves deeper into our caves, whether we view those differences through the lens of gender, age, sexuality, racial characteristics, beliefs or physical and mental abilities. We may find it difficult to accept or understand the experiences of those who are different from us, and might resent the adjustments we have to make to support their inclusion. Worse still, we might consider them– and those who do not fit into the boxes we have constructed – to be less than us, or indeed less than human.

Jory Fleming, speaking on the BBC News in May 2021 about his new book *How to be Human: An Autistic Man's Guide to Life* reminds us that before any conversations can begin, we must first recognise each other as humans, each with contributions to make.

Thus we have to constantly 'do the work' in challenging our biases and prejudices, starting with recognition, acceptance and a commitment to change. This requires a willingness to make adaptations and convert any 'square-box' thinking into different inclusive shapes, to make way for new ways of thinking and new ways of working. It takes a willingness to respond to new people and new environmental factors and adapt accordingly.

We need to keep the wheels of diversity, equity and justice turning

In 2021, Alexander McLean, attorney and founder of Justice Defenders (an organisation based in Uganda that supports imprisoned people in Africa), was asked on CNN Amanpour about his 'mixed background' (Jamaican father and English mother). He explained that perhaps such a background:

> *... equips us to act as bridges between people of different colours, statuses and backgrounds to ask: what does it look like to mix with people from different backgrounds? The world is crying out for this after George Floyd's death. Here at Justice Defenders, we are proud to believe in those that others have rejected, and recognise their talents and to love them as they serve their sentences and communities with dignity and compassion.*

The concept of empathy and the importance of building bridges of empathy within communities, while supporting others to do the same, is central to the *Six Stages Framework*. It requires an ability to see humanity in each and every one of us, regardless of differences – racial or otherwise – and to be able to recognise everyone's unique talents and potential.

The work in embracing racial equity and inclusion needs to start in schools

In March 2021, the UK Government Commission report on racial and ethnic disparities recognised that:

> *Younger ethnic minority people in the UK may identify more strongly with their ethnicity and heritage than older generations, reflecting a new desire to adopt multiple identities rather than 'to assimilate'. ... Strong ethnic identities should also not be considered in and of themselves as an inherent obstacle to British National building. People are evidently capable of juggling multiple identities in their everyday lives. What matters is for the British identity to evoke positive emotions of trust and affection in the country's minorities.*

In an article about supporting children and young people to embrace 'multiple identities', Elizabeth Kitto (2020) discussed how schools can tackle racism by teaching and helping children to see themselves holistically.

> *The future will be easiest for young people who can embrace diversity, as well as find common ground within it. Fear of something alien is quite natural. There is no malice*

in a child seeking friendships with people whom they believe share their values. However, by encouraging self-definition in a number of ways, we could help young people to reinforce social ties and demystify aspects of other cultures. This can mean they move between groups more freely, due to a collective sense of belonging.

If children are to be supported to identify and embrace (or even develop) multiple identities, then developing and embracing diversity and inclusion is a key to the process. It is important to build trust between all people, regardless of their ethnic background or other differences. It is important to teach them how to embrace those differences and to understand, recognise and challenge racism. This raises questions about how values can transpire from school leadership to classrooms, from children to the community, and from the present to the future.

As I wrote this, I was reminded of some young girls who, having left an independent school for girls (rated academically in the top three in the UK), wrote in 2020 to their headteacher and challenged her for not having prepared them sufficiently for society or for embracing diversity. As people marched the streets in the USA and UK calling for racial equity and justice, these girls called for the introduction of a black curriculum in schools, and for schools to better prepare future generations of students to understand and embrace diversity. The letter was signed by hundreds of current and past pupils. This school has mostly white English pupils. I previously raised concerns with the headteacher about friendships and the lack of inclusion of ethnic minorities; she made it clear to me that she did not see it as her or the school's responsibility to promote diversity or encourage young people to diversify their friendships; she considered this was the role of the parents. When asked about how the school could support pupils who felt isolated, the deputy head responded, "We can't just magic up friends".

In my view, it is the role of schools to teach and support young people to develop and embrace differences and diversity. Indeed, young people themselves are now complaining that their schools have failed them – have failed to adequately prepare them to engage fully and successfully in a multicultural and diverse society. It is ironic that, as a society, so much emphasis is placed on academic qualifications and so little on teaching about racial tolerance and equity and preparing our children for the world in which they are going to live as adults. These young people will succeed where 'we' have failed. I hope this headteacher will actually listen to their voices and feedback about their experiences.

Twenty years ago, little emphasis was placed on teaching children about recognising, understanding and managing their feelings and emotions (i.e. the emotional curriculum). I was one of the pioneers in developing training for schools and local authorities in this area. I called for training for teachers and educational psychologists to promote work related to emotional literacy and emotional intelligence in schools (M'gadzah, 2011).

In the years to come, I hope that teaching children about valuing differences, embracing diversity and inclusion, and understanding and challenging racism will be a key component of the curriculum. I also hope that work engaging boys and men in conversations about masculinity and domestic violence – as well as on creating a society in which girls and women feel safe and can walk alone at night without fear – will be commonplace. This requires us to recognise the humanity in every one of us. If we are to truly embrace DEI, we all need to support the management and nurturing of young people's identities in a modern world. We also need to do the same for employees in the workplace.

Work should continue into universities and teacher-training courses

In recent times, many have asked what universities are doing to address these issues. Is decolonising the curriculum the answer? McKie (2020) outlined some of the challenges and oppositions put forward for decolonising the curriculum and the reasons for maintaining the status quo, while Hopkinson (2020) considered the history of racism in the wake of the murder of George Floyd in the US and the subsequent outcry. He explored today's misconceptions of 'racism', stating:

> *Ignore populists and simplistic definitions; history should be central to our understanding of racism.*

Tuck and Wayne-Young (2012) bring attention to how settler colonialism shaped schooling and educational research in the US and other nation states. They highlight how more needs to be done in this area, rather than offering empty promises of decolonisation and reconciliation between institutions and indigenous peoples. They remind us that true decolonisation involves a relinquishing of power by these institutions to the indigenous peoples from which it was taken.

From my conversations on race with university students (M'gadzah, 2020), it is clear that they believe more must be done in this area, as do the young women at the independent school described above. They want clear facts and information that accurately reflects historical events. Above all, they are calling for a fairer society and for racial equity and justice.

The recent interview of the Duke and Duchess of Sussex, Prince Harry and Meghan Markle, with Oprah Winfrey polarised the world; young people under the age of forty seem to have more empathy for Harry and Meghan while the older generation is loyal to the rest of the Royal family. Some accused the couple of being disloyal to the Royal family; others said it is possible to be loyal to the Queen and yet still raise concerns about how the monarchy deals with racial differences, racism and mental health.

It is clear from these discussions that some of the values and attitudes of the past are being slowly questioned and the wheels of change are turning. This pull, between values and attitudes of the past, is also evident within workplaces; we are having to adapt to new ways and models of working post Covid-19 (McKinsey, 2021). The ability to change and adapt is becoming increasingly important for both individuals and organisations in many areas, including in the area of diversity and inclusion.

The *Six Stages Framework* shows us that we should be able to have discussions about racial differences and racism without conflict and without becoming polarised. Many are also asking what universities can do to promote safety for girls and women and to challenge misogyny and violence.

What is clear from these challenges of racism and misogyny is that we need to remove the responsibility for solving these issues from women and black and ethnic minority groups. In 2020, I set up an online group called Diversity, Equity, Inclusion & Psychology Network. Some young people joined this group and I truly believe that they – the future generation – will continue to call for more change. The current Covid-19 pandemic and the focus on racial equity and inclusion have shown how refreshing it is to have young people's views.

Conversations about race facilitate rich discussions that can contribute to and drive forward positive change. The starting point for this change is within our own homes and communities. We must not be afraid to have these conversations; instead, we should see them as a potential for growth. We must not underestimate the power of meaningful conversations and how we can all learn and influence each other and influence society for the greater good.

This has to be about more than just racial equity and inclusion—we must all take responsibility for change

I am still haunted by the news footage of George Floyd's tragic murder which shows him gasping for breath on the ground, and by the protests that followed around the world. As a psychologist interested in human behaviour, I truly believe (M'gadzah, 2020) that:

> *Without empathy and compassion we are nothing but animals.*

In his final essay (2020), US Congressman John Lewis reflected on hearing Dr Martin Luther King speak. Dr King reminded us all to stand up and speak out against the injustices we see:

> *Each one of us has a moral obligation to stand up, speak up and to speak out. When you see something that's not right you must say something, you must do something.*

Dr Lewis called upon us all before he died in 2020:

> *... a call to act as higher angels with courage, conviction and truth. We need to be able to show empathy and compassion to each other regardless of political party, race, gender or sexuality. We are all complicit when we tolerate injustice. It is not enough to say we will get better by and by. More importantly we need to show empathy and compassion even when others have failed to show us that in return.*

Ruth Bader Ginsburg (RBG) expressed similar sentiments in 1972 when she spoke up for the equality of women, long before it was fashionable to do so. In 1972, she co-founded the Women's Rights Project at the ACLU (American Civil Liberties Union). In 1993 she paid tribute to her mother, saying:

> *I pray that I may be as a Justice what my mother might have been if my mother might have lived in an era when women could be appreciated and could aspire, and their daughters were as cherished as their sons.*

When asked on the BBC News in 2020, 'What would you say to young women who look at your example and are either despondent in the current climate of social and racial injustice or feel that change is not be possible?', she replied:

> *Young people are my hope. My granddaughter is doing what she can to make things better in our society; think of @Malala and @GretaThunberg. I think at least the young people I see are fired up and they want our country to be what it should be. My faith, one of the things that makes me an optimist are the young people.*

RBG's words resonate with me and I strongly believe young people will demand more from us in making the world a just and more equitable place. While there may be some who will insist on things staying the same – saying this is the way we have always done things – most young people will demand more. It's as if they are able to view the world through a different lens, one that is devoid of the biases and discrimination that so many have suffered from.

Moving beyond fear towards racial equity and inclusion

We need to move beyond our fear of discomfort as individuals and as organisations if we are to make meaningful change is these areas. Ben Hecht, the CEO of Living Cities (2020), shared some of the playbook that his organisation had found valuable with other executives of Fortune 500 companies. His messages are clear:

> *Focus on the right things and move beyond their fear. The vast majority affirmed that racial equity was an obvious business imperative. But less obvious was what to do about it. With traditional diversity interventions failing, these leaders – the majority of whom were white – reported feeling ill-equipped, even afraid, to act.*

In his article on moving beyond diversity toward racial equity, Hecht stated:

> *Achieving racial equity in the workplace will be one of the most important issues that companies will tackle in the coming decade.*

He explained that consumers and employees do not want to see vague platitudes but rather see their organisations committing to real action.

Talking about his own company, Living Cities, he described how staff had informed him that it was a hard place to work for people of colour:

> *Despite a racially diverse staff, our office culture dictated that people of colour only contribute in ways that white people, including me, were comfortable with.*

He also described how project leaders dismissed the personal experiences of staff as being 'too emotional'. The view taken by the organisation was that discussions on racism were 'divisive' or 'unproductive' and they were therefore discouraged. This meant that the workplace was unable to acknowledge the lives lived by people of colour and value them for who they were. He reflected on the legacy of racism, which he described as:

> *... complex, brutally ugly, deeply personal, and yet to be truly reckoned with, especially in the workplace.*

He also acknowledged that the harmful effects of racism still live on:

> *... within our institutions and in each of us.*

The inclusion tools and practices of the 1990s were:

> *... grossly insufficient for racial equity work.*

They were less about driving fundamental changes within organisations and more about 'velcro-ing' guidelines, practices and programmes into existing structures and cultures of the workplace – all in an attempt:

> *... to help employees of colour better 'fit in' and succeed.*

He continued:

> *Today's racial equity and inclusion efforts must flip that premise on its head. Instead of trying to change some people to fit the organization, we must focus on transforming our organizations to fit all people. What I've realized over the six years since that initial, very difficult conversation with my staff is that our culture was the problem and had to be changed. To move toward racial equity, organizational culture must prioritize humanity. People need the ability to work with the dignity of having their histories acknowledged and their life experience valued. Only then will companies be able to recruit and retain the thriving, diverse workforce that leaders and customers want – and need – in the next decade, and beyond.*

Creating safe spaces for exploring values, beliefs, attitudes and behaviours

Exploring our beliefs and values helps us to examine our attitudes, behaviours and relationships to others including those who are different from ourselves. However, this process requires trust, empathy, compassion and – above all – letting go of the fear. It requires a willingness to embrace that which is different and work together for the sake of our communities and humanity. This work requires us to first understand and acknowledge our limitations; only by doing so can we inspire change, grow and achieve a common sense of shared purpose and belonging.

The first step in the process is showing a willingness to do the work and recognising that, in order to achieve racial equity and justice (and gender equity and safety for women, etc.), things have to change in society.

Individuals and organisations have to be prepared to do the hard work of 'taking a lens' to their values, beliefs and attitudes, and of looking long and hard at their relationships with those who are different.

To do this, we have to create safe and secure spaces. We need to be able to listen to the experiences of those who are different, open ourselves up to introspection and be prepared to get uncomfortable. We need to be able to accept support and challenges from others; most importantly, we have to be willing to take responsibility and to change.

Cultural changes in how we view things and do things are essential. It is only in this way that we can move forward and begin the transformation from positions of ethnocentric existence and entitlement to ones of embracing equity, diversity, inclusion and social integration.

The process involves identifying what changes need to happen at individual and organisational levels and putting in place action plans to work on achieving the outcomes identified. It is critical that we support professionals to evaluate and challenge their biases. Agarwal (2020) reinforced this, stating:

> *In times like this it's essential we become aware of the ways in which we are biased – so it doesn't become prejudice.*

In 2016, the economist, Heather McGhee (2021), introduced viewers of US television's C-Span Public Affairs Network to a caller named Gary who 'bravely' asked for her help in confronting his racism and prejudice. We need to be able to move to a position where these kind of conversations become commonplace and are no longer seen as 'brave'.

Author Afua Hirsch said about her book:

> *Our country is at a pivotal moment. ... Britain is a nation of unanswered questions, of avoided subjects of contradiction. We still refuse to shine a spotlight on race and identity or to explore the murky depths of our relationships with those who look physically different. Why don't we ask those questions? What is it that we are so afraid of?*

The *Six Stages Framework*, with its focus on creating safe spaces, acknowledges the fear and discomfort that many people feel when engaging with this type of work and provides a space for exploring these issues with a no-blame approach – one filled with compassion, empathy and understanding. In his 2020 article, Hecht stated:

> *Understanding that this was going to be a learning journey that would require me and all my staff to stretch ourselves gave me permission to focus on learning about race and racism, managing discomfort, and building competencies to distinguish between real danger worthy of panic and stretch-induced fear. ... To help staff and leadership become more comfortable with conflict, we use a comfort-stretch-panic framework which helps assess your own state of mind and physiological reactions when facing challenging moments. ... This work is hard and takes a deeply personal*

> *toll. The process is only as good as the commitment, trust, and goodwill from the staff who engage in it – whether that's confronting one's own white fragility or sharing the harms that one has experienced in the office as a person of color over the years.*

He further explained that in order to build new, more inclusive cultures, it is important to first see:

> *... the norms, values and practices in our institutions that advantage white people and ways of working, to the exclusion and oppression of all others.*

In order to do this effectively, it is essential for organisations to commit resources and time to staff's individual learning. It is critical that, as with all elements of management, organisations measure progress and adapt based on data.

In addition, Hecht stated that organisations need to ask the following questions:

> *How well equipped are staff to identify and address interpersonal, institutional, and structural racism in the workplace? How often are staff taking risks and putting aside discomfort to engage in critical conversations? How much does organizational leadership participate in and support conversations about racial equity internally?*

To conclude, he stressed the urgency of this work and highlighted the importance of not entering into such work lightly:

> *Organizations cannot afford not to do this work, but they also can't enter into it lightly, under the misconception that a training or workshop checks the box. True racial equity and inclusion work in the workplace must look unlike anything we've done in past decades, because we've consistently failed to tackle racial inequity at its deepest roots. But we can start today, by bringing our fullest selves to the offices and desks where we spend most of our waking lives and empowering each other to do the same.*

The *Six Stages Framework* provides a new way of tackling racial equity and inclusion work 'at its deepest roots'. It requires individuals to accept responsibility for doing the work, to take ownership and to show up as their 'fullest selves' when 'doing the work'. This level of commitment will afford them a new learning experience which starts in the home, school and community and can be transferred into the office, transforming the way they relate to those who are different and enabling them to let go of their fear.

3

Why use the *Six Stages Framework*?

The *Six Stages Framework* is designed specifically to promote our understanding and ability to deal with racism in a safe space. It:

- supports people as they learn to understand, recognise and challenge prejudice, misconceptions and stereotypes
- explores and identifies beliefs, values and behaviours of both individuals and organisations
- supports the exploration of learned attitudes, which are at the root of racism
- enables individuals to review the learned responses that are often a reflection of these attitudes
- acknowledges that racism exists in all racial groups and at all levels of society, and that basic survival instincts or social constructions (learned responses) are often at the root of racism
- supports individuals to evaluate their biases and make necessary adjustments
- supports individuals and organisations to explore how to manage and nurture identities in a modern world
- defines steps for coming out of 'caves of privilege' and entitlement
- supports individuals and organisations to generalise their learning into promoting diversity and inclusion in other areas where discrimination and inequity exist.

Commitment to this framework enables individuals and organisations to embark on a unique journey by identifying where they are in the developmental model. It encourages growth mindsets and allows strategies and action plans to be formulated for moving from each of the six stages to the next.

4

How does the *Six Stages Framework* approach racial equity and inclusion issues?

The *Six Stages Framework* was designed to provide support and challenge individuals and organisations in their efforts to combat racial inequity and racism. It is no ordinary framework, and the training provided is no ordinary training, because it puts emphasis on 'experiential' learning, and on stretching people and supporting them to manage their discomfort in a safe environment in which they are encouraged to engage in small-group tasks and activities (rather than 'normal' learning environments, in which they just listen to someone speaking or share their lived experiences).

The framework explains that racism exists within all racial groups and across all sectors of society, regardless of socioeconomic status. It emphasises the natural pull towards 'sameness' and towards people and situations that are 'comfortable' – both of which can be framed in the context of 'evolutionary programming'. However, racism is often about power, and it usually relates to attempts to remain within 'caves of privilege'.

The first steps of the programme are designed to allow individuals and organisations to determine where they are in terms of their awareness, understanding and responses to racism, and avoids 'blame' by pointing out that everyone is at a different point on their journey. It embraces the premise that participants need to understand racism and identify and explore their own beliefs, values, attitudes and behaviours before challenging their own (and others') prejudices and attempting to reform their views.

To progress through the stages of the programme, participants must first recognise where they are placed within the developmental stages of the framework. They are provided with an implicit-bias self-report questionnaire that they must complete, and will receive feedback including radar charts to help them visualise which of the six stages they are at.

Following this, they are coached about the processes they can use to support them as they progress through the stages of the developmental framework.

By committing to the framework, they are taught ways to confront their biases and prejudices, thus enabling them to begin the journey towards taking action against inequity, racism and racial injustice.

However, for this to work, they must be prepared to be open to uncomfortable conversations and be willing to explore and challenge their own perceptions of the world. Those who succeed often experience a paradigm shift and real transformation in how they relate to those who are different. This transformation is of benefit to both sides.

The *Six Stages Framework* supports individuals throughout this process and give them strategies for 'calling out' incidents involving racial inequity and racism. It helps them explore issues like 'strategic' racism – the type of racism that is often used in the political arena to trigger anxiety among white people (Lopez, 2021).

One example of this is ex-President Donald Trump, who is known for making racially polarising comments for fearmongering. The framework also enables individuals to create action plans to support them on their journey. For some, this may begin with simple actions, like getting to know a black or minority ethnic person if they don't already know one, or reading a relevant book, perhaps about white privilege or race and discrimination.

The framework is developmental in nature and can be viewed as a tool for promoting a 'growth' mindset, whereby anyone's basic abilities can be developed through dedication and hard work, creating openness to learning, self-development and a specific kind of resilience for exploring and challenging racism and inequity while supporting others to do the same.

Key aspects of the framework include:

- diversity assessments specially designed to explore attitudes, biases and behaviours
- coaching and support to promote learning and self-development
- engagement in conversations about differences and racism
- owning up to negative automatic thoughts
- looking beyond unconscious bias
- building bridges of empathy
- moving beyond diversity towards anti-racism and racial equity
- promoting diversity of thought
- recognising our own entitlement and coming out of 'caves of privilege'
- creating safe spaces
- recognising unhelpful/implicit beliefs and behaviours
- promoting strength-based resilience
- neurodiversity counselling and culturally competent therapy
- understanding leadership values
- exploring the role of white allies and allyship
- perspective-taking and developing emotional intelligence
- facilitating learning through role-play and scripts.

The role of emotional intelligence (EQ)

Emotional intelligence is an important part of the framework, and the training considers issues like:

- How do we support people to emerge from their caves?
- How do we engage and ask them questions?
- How do we make sure they do not blame themselves?
- How can they speak in an emotionally intelligent way?
- How can we help them perceive, use, understand and manage their own emotions and to self-regulate when talking about biases and racial differences? ?
- How do we help them take a lens to their beliefs and behaviours and alter their thinking?

The approach of the framework has been specifically designed to promote individuals' self-awareness and ability to understand, manage and regulate their emotions and behaviours effectively. It aims to enhance social awareness and the ability to understand the emotions of others by accurately perceiving and interpreting emotional cues. It focuses on emotional intelligence and social skills such as empathy (and compassion), which are discussed below.

5

What are the stages of the *Six Stages Framework*?

The six stages of the framework operate on a spectrum from +1 to +6 on a positive axis, and the assessments currently focus on supporting people to understand the progression up through these stages. However, the stages also exist on a negative axis, from –1 to –6. If someone progresses down the negative axis, it means their views and attitudes about those who are different are becoming negatively entrenched. The stages are developmental in nature and build on each other, so anyone at stage –5 will also exhibit the views and behaviours of those at the preceding stages.

Stages +1 and +2 on the positive axis mirror stages –2 and –1 on the negative axis. For someone at these stages, it is possible to move up the positive axis, showing increasing awareness of racial equity and justice and a willingness to change, or to move down the negative axis, indicating the deeper entrenchment of negative positions, views and possibly behaviours. There is less detail on the negative axis as it is currently only included to illustrate the dynamic and polar-opposite nature of the conceptual framework.

The *Six Stages Framework* tool can be used with anyone, regardless of their ethnicity, colour, racial background or other characteristics, to explore their understanding and ability to deal with racism. Even some black, Asian and other ethnic minority people will be at Stage +1 and head upwards on a positive trajectory to stage +6. Equally, there will be some who are on stage –1, who move down on a negative trajectory to stage –6, where their views of those who are a different colour or culturally different from them and their views of racism become entrenched.

The framework can also be used to support those who are experiencing discrimination and/or racism to explore their own understanding of the issues, and to explore their ability and capacity to deal with racism.

On the positive axis, individuals start at stage +1, with little appreciation of how racism operates; they can then move up to stage +6, to obtain a greater understanding of racism and to become more adept at challenging it. When faced with racism, those at this stage will have a greater capacity for dealing with it, by drawing upon their understanding of racism and how it operates.

On the negative axis, individuals start at stage −1, with little appreciation of how racism operates – some may not have even considered that racism exists and are therefore more vulnerable when they experience it. Those on the negative axis can move down to stage −6, and become overwhelmed in the face of their experiences and their views about those who are different. When faced with racism, they may feel totally powerless (more so than those on the positive axis) and their capacity to deal with their experiences is limited. They are likely to be even more traumatised by their experiences than those on the positive axis, with more damaging long-term effects to their self-esteem.

The six stages of the negative axis

The six stages of the negative axis are shown in Fig. 1 and explained in more detail below.

Stage −6: Extremists/leadership

People who are at this stage have strong racist views and work to champion them to others and recruit others to join them. They are likely to pose a risk of terrorism, extremism and violence. They create false narratives and world views that they 'sell' to others.

Stage −5: Entrenched views and behaviours

People at this stage exhibit strong racist views and enjoy sharing them with others. They try to persuade others of their point of view. Their views are extreme and can be verbally aggressive and threatening. They demonise people who are different, and may be a danger to the community and anyone who is different.

Stage −4: Anger and blaming of ethnic minorities

These people are likely to attack and reject the views of those who are different. Their ways of thinking may be, or may become, more extreme, and they may blame those who are different for their plight.

They use gaslighting techniques (a form of psychological manipulation) by attempting to sow seeds of doubt in their victims' minds, to make them question their own beliefs, and leaving them feeling anxious and overly sensitive about their situation. They can make them so anxious, in fact, that other people may view them as having a 'chip on their shoulder' or a victim mentality, or of 'crying racism'.

People at this stage are likely to believe, for example, that their jobs are being taken away from them or that their country is being taken over (and they want their country back). They tend to believe false narratives, conspiracy theories and world views, and, as they believe that this is 'where they fit or belong', it can take hold of their imagination, so they are at risk of being radicalised and groomed by those at stages −5 and −6.

Fig. 1: Linear representation of the negative axis of the Six Stages Framework.

–1	–2	–3a	–3b	–4	–5	–6
Lacks awareness Is oblivious Stays silent Is in denial Diverts to other topics rather than racial injustice	Is dismissive and avoidant of issues of race Is in denial Pretends that racial injustice and racism do not exist Increasingly distrustful and blaming of those who are racially different	Resentful of time spent on issues of race Displays outrage while projecting own racism on to others Swayed by conspiracy theories	Attacks and rejects those who are racially different Rejects terms like unconscious bias and micro-agressions	Becomes more extreme and intolerant of those who are racially different Blames those who are racially different for their plight Is in danger of becoming radicalised or being groomed	Exhibits strong racist views Shares views with others to influence them Is at risk of extremism and violence	Is able to take on a leadership role and negatively influence others Is at risk of extremism, violence and terrorism

Stage –3: Attacking and rejecting

Common features of people at this stage include resenting time spent on issues about racial differences and inequity, with displays of outrage or projection of their own racism onto others. They may believe conspiracy theories about racism, and argue that it does not exist. They may accuse those who complain of racism of having a 'victim mindset' and of remembering a time when racism was 'a lot worse than it is'. They may verbally attack others (including victims) who raise issues about racism, and use racist stereotypes in their conversations. Typical comments and beliefs they might express are:

- *Why do black lives matter when all lives matter?'*
- *Black protesters are violent and therefore they do not get my empathy or compassion.*
- *We are not racist and we deserve an apology for the criticism that has been levelled at us!*

They accuse those who call out racism of 'race-baiting nonsense', and may reject the existence of racist intent, arguing that it is racist to accuse someone else (and/or their supporters) of being racist. They may go as far as to demand apologies from others, which can trigger resentment and create further division between different parties, setting up a 'them versus us' situation (depending on who agrees with them).

They are likely to be swayed by conspiracy theories about racism and argue that it does not exist; they may reject terms like 'microaggression' and 'unconscious bias', stating they are 'unscientific'.

Stage –2: Dismissive and avoidant

People who are at this stage are aware of race issues, but they are often dismissive about them and may believe that racial inequity and social injustice are not big issues.

They may exhibit denial (and avoidance) of racial injustice, telling themselves and others that there are far more important inequalities and injustices in the world. They are more comfortable discussing other issues, like gender and disability, and point out inequalities other than racism. The denial and discomfort that arises from this leads to avoidance, resistance and anger, and shifts attention away from racism to other issues that they find more manageable and tolerable.

They often believe that racism occurs in other countries from their own, so it really isn't an issue for them. They respond to others' claims or concerns about racism by making excuses and being dismissive. They find reasons to explain away racial discrimination, to dismiss it and play it down, perhaps by stating that no harm was intended by someone's comments, or that their comments were merely dumb, or taken out of context, thus suggesting that the complainants are over-reacting (demonstrating a 'victim mindset'), of having 'negative narratives' and of remembering a time when racism was 'a lot worse than it is now'.

They avoid facing race issues, which distinguishes them from people at stage –1, who are oblivious and ignorant of the issues. While they have a sense that something is wrong, they push it down because it's too uncomfortable for them to face.

However, they may also be going through a quiet awakening about racial injustice, feeling uncomfortable about what they see and hear, even though they find ways to justify it to themselves. Conversations on the topic make them feel anxious and they try to avoid them. Their learned responses reflect their attitudes and they say things like:

- *I don't see colour.*
- *Racism is not an issue.*
- *Black people and other ethnic minorities do quite well in society.*

Stage –1: Unaware with silence and denial

Anyone at this stage is characterised by a lack of awareness of racial equity or diversity issues, often presenting as ignorant or being oblivious or ethnocentric. Their learned responses often reflect their attitudes, and they say things like:

- *I'm not racist; one of my mates is black.*
- *I love all coloured people.*
- *I don't see colour'.*

They may be silent or deny race issues, perhaps by keeping their head down and hoping a conversation will end, or by diverting a discussion to another subject that seems safer. Some of them believe that issues of racial injustice are unimportant, displaying an ethnocentric perspective, and exhibiting aversion-type behaviours including avoidance of social integration.

The six stages of the positive axis

The six stages of the positive axis are shown in Fig. 2 and explained in more detail below.

Stage +1: Unaware, silence and denial

These people lack awareness of racial equity and diversity issues, often coming across as being ignorant or oblivious. There is silence or denial of the issues, and they keep their heads down, hoping conversations will end, possibly diverting them to some other 'safer' topic. Some may believe that issues of racial and social injustice are unimportant. Their perspective tends to be ethnocentric and they may show aversion-type behaviours and avoid social integration. Often they don't see racial inequity or racism, and have learned responses that are a reflection of their attitudes and ignorance. Typically they may say:

- *I don't see colour.*
- *Racism is not an issue.*

They are more likely to share anecdotes about their experiences of people from ethnic minorities that are based on stereotypes, perhaps relating to a recent holiday, the friendliness of such groups, or what lovely smiles they have (e.g. 'smiles that can light up a whole room').

Stage +2: Dismissive and avoidant

People who are at this stage are aware of race issues, but often dismiss them or deny them, believing that racial inequity and social injustice are not big issues. They tell themselves (and others) there are far more important inequalities and injustices to consider.

They feel discomfort and anxiety which leads to avoidance, resistance and anger, and they try to shift attention away from racism to other issues that they find more manageable, such as gender and disability. This may be because they are experiencing a quiet awakening, and are beginning to feel uneasy about what they see and hear. They may have an inkling something is wrong but push such thoughts away, instead finding ways to justify such things and avoiding uncomfortable conversations. Often their learned responses reflect their attitudes and lack of understanding. Typically they say things like:

- *I'm not racist – one of my mates is black.*
- *I love all coloured people.*
- *I don't see colour.*
- *Black people and other ethnic minorities do quite well in society.*

This group differs from people at stage +1 because they avoid race issues, rather than being oblivious to or ignorant of them. Often they like to believe that racism occurs in other countries, rather than their own country. Their responses to claims of racism are to make excuses to justify why there cannot be racial discrimination or racism, and may take the stance, for example, that no harm was intended by their comments – that their comments were dumb, unintended, or taken out of context – and may suggest that the complainant over-reacted, to play down the issues. Further, they may accuse complainants of having a 'victim mindset' and referring to a time when racism was 'a lot worse than it is'.

Stage +3: Becoming aware of issues of race

Here, people are becoming more aware of differences and racism, questioning the stances they held at stages +1 and +2. They may recognise inequity and racism but do not understand why or what they can do about it, feeling uncomfortable talking about them, and possibly overwhelmed. They may also feel helpless or guilty, even shame, perhaps demonstrating a desire to make things okay for everyone. Often they view themselves as advocates, and talk about how hard it must be for those who are different, and report knowing someone who is different, yet remain unaware of their own biases and behaviours. They are awakening to issues of injustice they encounter, for example in the media, and may discuss with interest current issues about racial injustice they've

Fig. 2: Linear representation of the positive axis of the Six Stages Framework.

Stage	Characteristics
+1	Lacks awareness Presents as ignorant Stays silent Is in denial Diverts to other topics rather than racial injustice
+2	Dismissive and avoidant of issues of race Pretends that racial and social injustice do not exist Is in denial Experiences a quiet awakening about racial injustice Begins to feel uncomfortable
+3a	Recognises that racial inequity and racism exist Expresses discomfort about issues of racism Experiences sense of helplessness and guilt Begins to own up to own biases and prejudices
+3b	Becomes more aware of issues of racism Questions original stance and perceptions Feels over-whelmed
+4	Becomes open to learning and having meaningful conver-sations that challenge own per-ceptions Challenges own and others' biases and prejudices about racism
+5	Is able to reflect and genuinely eng-age on issues of racism Begins to see the bigger picture about racial inequity (paradigm shift) Recognises own and others' uncon-scious biases Consistently speaks about and challenges discrimination and racism Understands that racism is about power and how this operates in organisations
+6	Is able to take on a leadership role in promoting equity and social justice Joins with others for the greater good and the sake of humanity Is able to recognise and challenge institutional racism and support others to do the same

heard about, or 'taking the knee', or Marcus Rashford discussing food poverty. Usually this is only done informally, among family, friends and close colleagues.

Stage +4: Open to learning

These people are genuinely open to learning and having meaningful conversations about race, including challenging perceptions and biases. They listen willingly and re-educate themselves, perhaps seeking out literature on the experiences and testimonials of black people and other ethnic groups, showing willingness to gain more understanding. They are likely to reflect and engage readily in conversations and will explore – and own – any unconscious bias they have. They freely share honest accounts of their own experiences and level of social integration. They are also open to concepts of privilege, including 'white privilege', and other positions of power. They are willing to work on any unintended microaggressions or biases.

Stage +5: Ability to see the bigger picture

This group of people are able to reflect and genuinely engage in conversations and issues of social and racial injustice and racism because they can see the bigger picture around race. They are capable of exploring and owning their unconscious bias, privilege status, or other positions of power informed by the reading and education they undertook in stage +4. Similarly, they are able to share honest accounts of their experiences and discuss levels of social integration. They may experience a paradigm shift.

Overall, they see a 'greater good' and the need to act for the sake of humanity. They speak up and challenge racism when they see it both within their personal lives and elsewhere, like in the workplace, and are keen to explore their role as an ally and discover more about how they can make a difference.

Stage +6: Leadership qualities

People at this final stage +6 may take on leadership roles to promote racial equity, inclusion and social justice. They may desire to join with others to challenge social injustice and racism, possibly through community engagement, in a greater cause, with the understanding that there is more that unites us than separates us.

They have genuine compassion and empathy, instead of a focus on the 'self' or on attitudes such as the potential for 'losing something' if and when things change (e.g. lose a position of privilege); they are willing to 'come out' of any cave of privilege with new-found resilience so that they can engage and interact with others in different ways.

They actively support others and appreciate the power of collaboration for the sake of humanity with the understanding that racism is about power and systems. So they focus their energies on supporting change in this area, and speak up to challenge racism or perceptions of racism when others are afraid to. They are clear about allyship and their role.

Bennett's developmental model of intercultural sensitivity (DMIS)

As I was writing this book I came across the Bennett (2007) Developmental Model of Intercultural Sensitivity (DMIS), which has many similarities with the framework described on these pages. They both outline how people react to cultural differences and both are based on concepts from cognitive psychology to constructivism. Interestingly, Bennett organised his observations into six stages too, with a progression of increasing sensitivity towards cultural integration. The Bennett Scale (as outlined in Fig. 3) is useful for helping organisations understand their journey through DEI, moving from centric perspectives to integrative relative transformations. Initially I was surprised by these similarities, but in reality it isn't surprising that two psychologists would come up with similar constructions, despite some real differences between them.

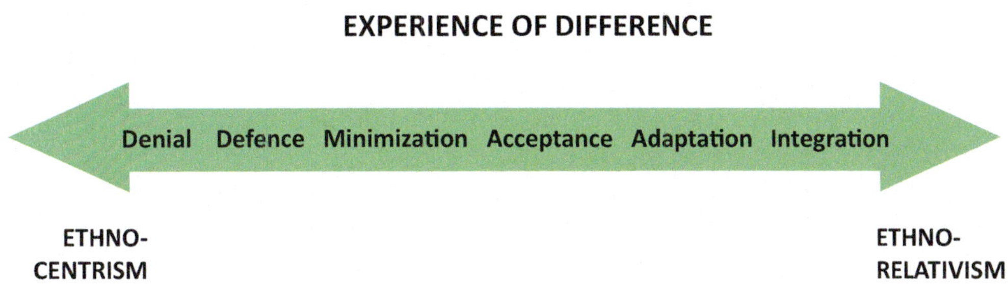

Fig. 3: The Bennett scale – a developmental model of intercultural sensitivity (DMIS). Adapted from Bennet 2007.

Hammer's cultural development continuum (IDC)

Dr Mitch Hammer developed the cultural development continuum (IDC) model, which was a further refinement of Bennett's DMIS model. It progresses from a monocultural mindset to an intercultural mindset, describing:

> *... a set of knowledge/attitudes/skill sets or orientations towards cultural difference but arrayed along a continuum from monocultural mindsets of Denial and Polarisation through the transitional orientation of Minimisation to the intercultural or global mindsets of Acceptance and Adaptation.*

The continuum includes the following:

- denial (misses differences)
- polarisation (judges differences)
- minimisation (de-emphasises differences)

- acceptance (deeply comprehends differences)
- adaptation (bridges across differences).

Again, there are similarities between this model and the *Six Stages Framework*, in as much as each shows a developmental progression towards greater 'acceptance' and 'adaptation'.

Wilber's integral theory

Ken Wilber's integral theory was published in 2005. It is useful in everyday life for helping individuals to develop in any activity, and to help them become 'comprehensive and effective' at it.

> *In short, the integral approach helps you see both yourself and the world around you in more comprehensive and effective ways.*

Wilber described the stages of emotional development and lines of development, and referred to the work of Carol Gilligan, an American psychologist, who described the stages of moral growth, which move from egocentric to ethnocentric to world-centric to integrated. These stages are hierarchical in nature:

> *Because each stage has a higher capacity for care and compassion.*

The *Six Stages Framework* is hierarchical in nature, whereby each stage shows a higher capacity for dealing with and understanding racism.

6

DEI issues—further exploration of psychosocial factors

For some, change is slow—others are tired and numb to the messages of DEI

It often seems that some people switch off from messages about racial equity and inclusion. Psychologists recognise that if someone experiences something often enough, they become numb and their feelings and responses are suppressed.

This certainly appears to be the case in the area of DEI. When we are bombarded with information, in this case about the lack of racial tolerance and acceptance of racial differences, and are told we have to change, some of us stop listening or responding to the messages and become numb to the suffering around us. Our brains filter out the information and we can switch off. However, at what cost do we do this? Events across the world warn us about the dangers of racism and intolerance of differences and what happens when a sense of privilege and entitlement remains unchecked.

After months of conversations about racial equity and inclusion (M'gadzah, 2020), it became clear to me that training and development work on racism often fails to catch peoples' attention, resulting in the messages being lost. While researchers have found some evidence for the effectiveness of 'unconscious' bias training for reducing unconscious bias and explicit bias (Equality Human Rights Commission, 2018), others continue to raise concerns about the efficacy of training (Zestcott *et al.*, 2016, Chang *et al.*, 2019) and whether it genuinely has an impact on changing beliefs and behaviour.

Some individuals consider it to be irrelevant to them. For instance, some Conservative MPs in the UK argue against it, protesting that it is equivalent to being 'told what to think' (Murphy and Walker, 2020).

However, the power of opening up conversations has never been clearer. Making space to share lived experiences and explore ways for 'building bridges of empathy', along with assessing our starting points as individuals and organisations, are the key ingredients for making meaningful changes. Feedback from those who have attended the *Six Stages Framework* programme confirms the importance of being provided with an evidence-based framework and an implicit-bias type questionnaire, along with guided support to promote change. What we need are Training courses and programmes that tackle the real issues — that are not afraid to engage people and organisations in honest, transparent and meaningful conversations.

I recently re-watched the film *The Color Purple*, based on the fictional book by Alice Walker (1982). I had first watched it many years ago, but I realise I had been too young back then to understand its messages. The issues it deals with are still very relevant today. Wikipedia described it this way:

> *Set in the early 1900s, it tells the story of a young African–American girl named Celie Harris and shows the problems African–American women faced during the early 20th century – domestic violence, incest, paedophilia, poverty, racism and sexism. Celie is transformed as she finds her self-worth through the help of two strong female companions.*

The book has been banned in some US schools because of its sexual content, explicit language and graphic depictions of violence, and it has been criticised for its stereotypical narratives of black male violence. Others find its representations compelling and relatable. I was struck by how some attitudes and behaviours towards women, black people and homosexuals depicted in the film are still very much the same today – just more covert. The view that speaking up as a black person, whether in the workplace or to a police officer, is not allowed was clearly portrayed by Oprah Winfrey's character, Sofia, when the white, moneyed character (married to the town's mayor), Miss Millie, said to her, 'Your kids are so clean. You wanna come work for me, be my maid?'. 'Hell no!' Sofia responded.

Sofia was beaten up, imprisoned and then forced to work as Miss Millie's maid – separated from her children for many years. Miss Millie (played by actor Dana Ivey) visited shops to buy presents for 'the poor coloured children' and purported to do charity work for them, while, ironically, having racist views. Some would say her attitudes and behaviours were a reflection of the times she was living in. When Celie's daughter was in Africa, she asked why her friend was not allowed to go to school and was told that girls there were not allowed to be educated. She commented:

> *That's just like back home in America where white people think black people should not be educated.*

Miss Millie's treatment of Sofia is evidence of the beliefs held by some people during those times, whereby black and ethnic minorities were considered unequal to white people and were expected to be subservient to them. I would argue that these views still exist today; they may not be expressed so overtly, but still hold true for some.

This is a brilliant illustration of how the past haunts the times we live in, not because black people cannot let go of it, but because some people still hold discriminatory and racist views reminiscent of those times – views that only really belong in the past. Yet a recent report for the UK Government (2021) claims that racist views are a thing of the past and those complaining of racism hold negative narratives.

We may have come a long way in the last fifty to one hundred years but biases and prejudices still exist. The difference is that such views are now considered to be socially unacceptable and are therefore rarely shared openly – but they may still be shared behind closed doors, and form the foundations of many people's self-constructed caves. We did, of course, see racist abuse and views out in full view following the UEFA Euro football finals (see below).

Going back to Miss Millie, she sometimes treated Sofia like a friend; she praised Sofia, telling her she was an excellent teacher when she taught her how to drive; and showing Sofia her emotions by getting upset in front of her, lamenting that she didn't know any of the other black people, so they couldn't drive her home! But nestled beneath all this remained her dominant view that Sofia was unequal – someone who should be subservient to her.

We see many 'Miss Millies' in society today – some of them even have black friends. But their beliefs and attitudes can betray those friendships. In truth, they do not consider black people as their equals and think they should really be 'their maids'. They consider black people subservient and often think they are there to 'entertain' them.

Unfortunately, opportunities rarely arise to talk about issues like these. Many people are not brave enough to share their beliefs (or fears) and have a spotlight shone on them. Therefore, their views continue to exist, burrowing further underground, perhaps inside their caves of privilege. This may be made worse if they only visit people who inhabit similar caves. Some attitudes are passed down from generation to generation, viewing those who are different as being less than human. These views continue to affect their behaviours and the ability to interact or integrate with people who are different.

What lengths do people go to minimise contact with people from other racial groups? What is the point of inclusive policies in the workplace?

In an article from June 2021, Fitzgerald discussed the extent that some white people will go to minimise contact and social interactions with people of other races. He mentioned a study by Jon Jachimowicz, an assistant professor in the Organizational Behavior Unit at Harvard Business School, and his publication titled 'Structuring local environments to avoid diversity: anxiety drives whites' geographical and institutional self-segregation preferences', in which he stated:

> *White people often take steps to avoid interacting with people of other races, whether it's at home, work, or even on a golf course ... White people often feel anxious about interacting with non-Whites, and they go out of their way to erect barriers to reduce contact with minorities, according to new research. ... And White people often attempt to erect barriers – even seemingly innocuous ones like stricter dress codes at golf and tennis clubs – to isolate themselves from minorities, according to research that involved surveying hundreds of people and studying thousands of datasets at government and social organizations.*

Quoting Jachimowicz, Fitzgerald described how this can "fuel a self-perpetuating cycle of segregation" and added:

> *... this not only affects intergroup relations but restricts the access of minorities to valuable resources primarily controlled by White people.*

He cited Jachimowicz again:

> *It's not that Whites always do this – but that when given the power and the opportunity, they may seek ways to reduce the racial diversity in the spaces they inhabit to lessen contact with racial minorities.*

Coming at a time when the cries for racial equity and justice have increased, Fitzgerald said:

> *Jachimowicz says it should be a 'call to action' for people and organizations to make substantive personal and professional changes to foster more positive connections among racial groups – interactions that studies have shown have the potential to reduce biased behaviors.*

He also referred to Jachimowicz's comments about business leaders:

> *... grappling with improving racial equity in the workplace the researchers report that important changes need to go beyond actively recruiting, hiring, and promoting more minority employees – and toward implementing workplace policies that challenge the self-segregation of White employees, which may occur if left unchecked.*

Fitzgerald posed a question: 'Are white people segregating consciously?', and explained that (according to Jachimowicz):

> *This anxiety-driven self-segregation can be seen across America in various towns, neighbourhoods, workplaces, school systems, social gatherings, and even tiny enclaves of White people in overwhelmingly diverse cities.*

Fitzgerald also stated:

> *The results raise an uncomfortable question: Are the self-segregating behaviors exhibited by many White Americans the result of conscious or unconscious racist thoughts?*

Jachimowicz (cited in Fitzgerald) responded to this question by explaining:

> *To me, that's a less important question, I think that what's more important is the outcome. Our research shows that, left to their own devices, many White people create barriers to limit intergroup contact. The fact is that we're all doing this one way or the other, and we're all responsible for the outcome. As a result, we all need to make changes in our lives.*

CNN News recently reported on the impact on white people of having contact with, or living next door to, black families, claiming, for example, that they are more likely to vote Democrat rather than Republican (2021). In an article published in June 2021, Annabel

Grossman reported that:

> *... socialization in early life may have long term effects on attitudes.*

The study of a 1940 census revealed that white boys who lived next door to black neighbours were more likely to be Democrats, even seventy years after leaving the neighbourhood. This study suggests that white men who grow up with black neighbours may have a more open-minded outlook in the future. Ryan Enos, a political scientist at Harvard University and one of the leading authors of the study cited by Grossman, said:

> *Ask how many more or less people would have different racial attitudes if we had a more or less segregated society at the time – it adds up to a lot.*

This self-styled segregation is something I experienced when working for a number of local authorities where I was the only black psychologist. During my time in these services, I was able to facilitate the recruitment of many black and ethnic minority psychologists to my teams, leading one manager to say, "I don't know how I feel about the fact that your area is the only area with a diverse workforce". What became clear is that when I was on interview panels, I was able to shine a light on the decision-making process and remove barriers that existed in the recruitment of black and ethnic minority psychologists, thereby increasing the diversity of my teams.

Many organisations, including Educational Psychology Services, often claim they have tried to recruit a more diverse workforce but with no success. They often fail to see the barriers that exist in their selection processes and recruitment policies, barriers they have consciously or unconsciously erected that result in the appointment of certain types of psychologists, who more closely resemble them.

Complacency and complicity sit in the shadow of silence

On the BBC News in June 2020, the UK Prime Minister, Boris Johnson, stated:

> *We are a much less racist society than we were and we are much happier and better for it. But we must also frankly acknowledge that there is much more to do in eradicating prejudice and in creating opportunities. And the government that I lead is committed to that effort.*

In July 2020, David Isaac, the Head of Equality and Human Rights Commission, criticised the government on the BBC News for dragging its feet over racism and failing to take meaningful action:

> *There is a need for a coherent strategy to tackle racism and businesses have to play their part in setting targets to recruit more people of colour into senior positions. There are unequal outcomes and black people are right to be concerned about their role and ability to be able to succeed. We need a coherent race strategy and a real need for leadership by the government. Covid has shown a real inequality in terms of*

> *outcomes for black people. Setting targets and putting in place programs to support black and ethnic minority staff to ensure that they flourish in the same way that other people flourish is key. Businesses must play their part too.*

Following the death of George Floyd, psychologists and many other professional groups have looked inward to dismantle racism within the field (Abrams, 2021). It's more than twenty years since Dr Simon Gibbs and I edited the British Psychological Society's (BPS) *Division of Education and Child Psychology* (DECP) journal (1999) on challenging racism within education and educational psychology. In 2015, in a special edition on racism, Williams *et al.* commented on how little had changed since that first publication:

> *In 1999, this journal produced a special edition 'Challenging Racism and Inequality in Education and Child Psychology' in which the editorial challenged Educational Psychologists (EPs) 'to critically review our practice, set ourselves targets (in EPSs, schools, training course, in recruitment and in the community) and review progress' (M'gadzah and Gibbs 1999, p.5.) It then seems long overdue to return to a consideration of educational psychology practice in relation to the diversity of the communities with whom educational psychologists work. This edition is an attempt to draw attention to the need to reflect on our effectiveness in acknowledging and addressing the experience of minority communities within educational psychology practice.*

In 'First letter to white educational psychologists: We can't breathe – black lives matter', published first on an online professional forum (M'gadzah, 2020), I posed the following question:

> *Honestly, hands up those of you who are relieved that the Black Lives Matter discussion thread seems to have ended and we can now move onto more important things or at least get back to normal?*

At that time, it seemed to me that the rest of the world and various professional groups were calling for racial justice and change, while others (including many psychologists) had moved past the discussion, and the thread described above, as if they were unperturbed by the lack of action or change. I could only assume they had convinced themselves it had nothing to do with them – despite being challenged by the statements of many ethnic minority colleagues and the voices of those taking part in the solidarity protests. I went on to say:

> *I suspect there will be many colleagues out there who have been holding their breaths waiting for things to return to 'normal', maybe saying that we just have to ride this particular storm and we will soon be back to our comfortable discussions, because discussions on racism will be over.*

Almost twenty months after George Floyd's death, I am still left asking: *What happens next? Where is the evidence of change?*

I ask this question of all professions and organisations that should be concerned, including those representing the Educational Psychology profession. Will we see real change? Or more working parties? Or, as the UK Prime Minister modelled in his response to the voices and outcry of those marching on the streets, the set up of another review or commission to collect yet more information? We already have plenty of evidence and information on racial inequity, injustice and racism – of how it impacts outcomes for black and ethnic minority groups. More importantly, we have yet to implement recommendations from previous government reviews and working parties!

When I wrote 'Second letter to white educational psychologists' on the Educational Psychology Forum (M'gadzah, 2020), I wondered why some psychologists couldn't be bothered to engage in these issues. Some of them stayed silent and didn't engage; others seemed highly anxious about the uncomfortable conversations; some were terrified of them. I appealed to my colleagues and stated:

> *There is a need to be open to engaging in much needed conversations on racism and equity issues affecting black and minority ethnic groups within society and the psychology profession. Black and minority ethnic psychologists and the future generation of psychologists deserve to know that they have been heard; that* ***the profession has reflected and taken action to ensure change*** *[author's emphasis]. They deserve to know that* ***psychologists did not hide in the shadows of silence, holding their breath until the Uncomfortable Conversations on Racism were over*** *[author's emphasis].*

Sally Casterton (2021) wrote candidly about the role of 'white allies'. I posted on LinkedIn in July 2021, signposting readers to her article and LinkedIn post in which she had asked:

> *What power do White allies have? Should White people feel comfortable in order for change to happen? Are statements enough or is there more that we should be doing? Inspired by the challenge laid down by Dr Shungu Hilda M'gadzah in her Clubhouse Everyday Psychology Club 'Dealing with Racism: The Six Stages Framework', I have written some reflections on the conversation that happened. The challenge was this – what can we do as individuals? Because conversation is key, but statements condemning racism are not enough.*

Casterton acknowledged the following:

> *Before committing myself to antiracism, I did not understand that I had any work to do or any role to play in ending racism, because I did not believe that I had ever taken any consciously racist actions. I did not realise how I was silently and unwittingly perpetuating the status quo by not acting to change myself and to change my corner of the world. ... The importance of allyship was raised during the discussion, with a reminder that so often White people have access to people and spaces that Black people do not. Here we can make a huge difference by persisting with conversations, making introductions, pressing for change, questioning policies, procedures, processes. Truly advocating for others not present to be heard – providing a voice in those spaces.*

She reinforced the fact that we need more people to take up positions as allies. However, for this to happen, we must recognise that self-reflection and self-awareness are key. The work starts with the self.

The UK Commission on Race and Ethnic Disparities Report 2021

In their 2021 report on race and ethnic disparities, the UK Commission claimed there is no evidence that the UK is 'institutionally racist'. It suggested that the UK should be seen as a model for other countries because claims of institutional racism are not borne out. The Black Lives Matter (BLM) movement in the UK criticised this long-awaited report on racism. They say it went out of its way to deny and obscure the existence of racism (John, 2021).

> *We are also disappointed to learn that the report overlooks disproportionality in the criminal justice system – particularly as police racism served as the catalyst for last summer's protests.*

The government report claimed that the UK is a 'model' for other white-majority countries – if so, some say, then they seem to have set the bar very low indeed. The CNN reporter, Tara John, informed us in her 2021 article that issues about racism are becoming "less important". Her report suggested that hate crimes are rising "because of improved police-recording processes, and a greater awareness of what constitutes a hate crime." She cited the founding director of Operation Black Vote, Simon Woolley, who said:

> *It is a monumental denial of structural racial inequality in the UK and, in fact, they're denying it even exists, which is frankly appalling.*

Tara John added:

> *Campaigners said the report was politicized and failed to adequately address a number of barriers that minority groups face in the UK, from job discrimination, to being disproportionately represented in the criminal justice system, or how minority ethnic frontline workers have died disproportionately during the Covid-19 pandemic.*

The UK Government Commission Report indicates to me that the UK is at stage +2 on the *Six Stages Framework* – or, worse still, stage −2, depending on whether they are heading upwards on the positive axis or downwards on the negative. Those at stage +2 may be dismissive about race issues, considering that racial inequity and social injustice don't exist, and trying to convince themselves and others that racial injustice is not an issue – that there are far more important inequalities and injustices in the world.

Their view is that black people and other ethnic minorities do quite well in society. They like to believe that racism occurs in other countries, like the USA, and not in their own country. To them, it really isn't an issue. Their default response to claims of racism is to make excuses and be dismissive of others' concerns, excuses that explain why there cannot be racial discrimination or racism. They may even go so far as to accuse those who complain of racism of having a 'victim mindset' and of living in the past and perpetuating 'negative narratives'. The Commission report reinforces the fact that individuals and organisations at these polar-opposite stages tend to make the same types of statements and exhibit the same types of behaviours. The list below is based on comments found in the report:

- They blame social media for amplifying racist views and online commentaries while trying to convince us that things are 'not so bad'.
- They believe that overly pessimistic narratives about race have been reinforced by the rise of identity politics.
- They blame so-called lobby groups for focusing on the lived experience of the groups they seek to protect and put less emphasis on objective data.
- They believe that mainstream public debates about race sensitise minorities to discrimination but do not highlight minority self-reliance or resilience.
- They accuse those who raise concerns about racism of not recognising improvements in outcomes for minorities and of not being open-minded, introducing a more fatalistic narrative that claims nothing has changed in relation to racial matters.
- They argue about a tendency to conflate discrimination and disparities, asserting that while they sometimes co-exist, they often do not.
- They argue that dominant narratives have a negative direction (such as racist abuse on social media) rather than a positive one.
- They believe there is repeated misapplication of the term 'racism' to account for every observed disparity.
- Despite the continued experiences and voices of minority groups, they believe that "attitudes towards racism and hate crimes have changed dramatically", and that those who do not agree are "undermining the apparent march of progress".
- They prefer to focus on racial disadvantage, asserting that, because it is possible to have racial disadvantage without racism, they need to look elsewhere for the roots of such disadvantage.
- They suggest that racial disadvantage often overlaps with social class disadvantage and argue that some groups have transcended this disadvantage more swiftly than others.
- They focus on the behaviours and attitudes among some people in minority groups that actively hold back integration, and say little about the behaviours and attitudes of white groups.
- They argue that racism is both real and socially constructed, yet say, "society has 'defined racism down' to encompass attitudes and behaviours that would not have been considered racist in the past" and that "This is one reason for the rise in sensitivity, the language of micro-aggressions and safety, and stretching the meaning of racism without objective data to support it."
- They make unsubstantiated statements such as: "almost exactly half of ethnic minority Briton's do not think that race has been an obstacle to their personal advancement," and "a majority of ethnic-minority Britons agree that race relations have improved over the last 50 years and this view is held by three times as many people as those who believe race relations have got worse."

- They argue that "although the continued presence of discrimination gives cause for concern, it is important to see how the UK has improved race relations more rapidly than in other countries."

The report fails to acknowledge the fact that previous definitions of racism may have been too narrow and limited. Instead, it focuses on criticising current definitions as including 'attitudes and behaviours' which would not have fallen into previous definitions. My view is that as our understanding of differences and racism advances, it can only be expected that definitions of racism will evolve too.

We cannot stem these changes, nor should we limit our understanding and ability to deal with racism. To say this cannot be racism, because it would not have fallen under the definition of it years ago, is the same as saying modern-day slavery is not wrong because it would not have been considered so according to the old definitions of human rights. The report also stated that:

> *In the UK the best way to build trust is to emphasize to every ethnic group that they will treat individuals fairly, and not on the basis of their ethnicity. We respect ethnic identities but also share a common, unifying, civic identity as British citizens.*

I find it disappointing that the UK Government thinks the best line of defence is to deny structural racism and blame the victims of it, questioning their self-reliance and resilience. This points the finger of blame at the victims, lobby groups, social media and lone parents – in other words, anywhere but the government! Here are two more quotes from the report:

> *If it is possible to have racial disadvantage without racists, then we need to look elsewhere for the roots of that disadvantage. To repeat: this is not about allocating blame, but simply pointing out that children require both time and resources, and that is more likely to be available when both parents play active roles in their upbringing.*

Nicholas Cheffings (2021), past global Chair of international law firm, Hogan Lovells (which focuses on advocacy for diversity, inclusion, anti-racism, equity and equality in business and society) commented on the report on LinkedIn:

> *Whatever positives might be found in some of the detailed recommendations, my initial reaction to the key themes that have hit the headlines is the same as that of every non-white person to whom I have reached out. They are people who are successful in their careers and none are (to quote from the report) reluctant to acknowledge that the UK has become more open and fairer than it was. Nor are they 'fatalistic', but none of them can match what they have read with what they experience. It is important to recognise this lived reality with #allyship, and it is vital that business leaders do not see this review (or that we are 'the model for other white-majority countries') as a reason to scale back efforts, believing we are doing fine. We aren't. We still have a long way to go. Now is the time to be working even harder to put right what is so obviously wrong.*

Understanding the true colours and nature of racism

In an article called 'Racism is not just a white problem – it's time we Asians confronted our own prejudices', Yasmin Alibhai-Brown (2020) discussed South-Asian prejudice and Asian anti-black racism. She revealed that she was:

> *... raised a racist and that trying to excise that scourge was a lifelong struggle ... British Asians found that upsetting to hear. Too bad. It is time.*

She also described the situation in the UK, USA and Uganda:

> *Black people, males in particular, are subjected to the most brutal race hate. The rest of us put up with exclusion, discrimination, threats and, increasingly, relentless abuse. Our disunities weaken our resistance and embolden neo-fascists and racists.*

Talking about her birthplace, Uganda, she said:

> *White and brown people subjugated indigenous Ugandans and used racist tropes to justify the structural inequality. We were in the middle of the human tree, with white people above us, and black people beneath us in every way.*

She talked of entrenched colour-coded and internalised colourism and xenophobia, which was previously outlined by Sunil Bhatia, a professor of human development at Connecticut College in the USA, who said:

> *There is a line that goes from in-group prejudices against members who are not fair-skinned, to racist recoil from people of African heritage.*

Alibhai-Brown also introduced us to Meena in her article, an Asian professional woman who is married to a black man. Describing Meena's current situation, she explained:

> *All these years on, she still hears insensitive comments from kith and kin about her mixed-race children, their curly hair and skin colour.*

Former BBC correspondent, Barnie Choudhury, spoke to Alibhai-Brown in 2020 about the ways in which racism is hidden:

> *In the communities I reported on, the racism is hidden and people try not to show their true colours. ... It's infuriatingly covert and cleverly hidden. ... But once they think you're one of them, they'll open up to you. You just need to know which buttons to press, and suddenly their prejudices come out. It's in the DNA.*

We have seen this with US Presidents, Nixon and Regan, in racist conversations that took place in 1971 (they thought they were alone), in which they disparaged African delegates to the United Nations (UN) (Naftali, 2019). This reinforces the fact that racist views exist within governments, and to pretend otherwise is disingenuous. What is needed is not denial of the existence of racism, but a commitment to talking openly about it and to making changes. The Oprah Winfrey interview with Meghan Markle and Prince Harry, and the responses that followed, seemed to indicate a reluctance of those within Buckingham Palace to understand the realities of everyday racism in the UK. Prince

Prince Harry said:

> *This wasn't just about her; it was about what she represents as a mixed-race person. I never expected it. I hadn't really thought about the mixed-race piece well. Firstly I've spent many years doing the work and doing my own learning. But my upbringing in the system which I've been brought up in, I wasn't aware of things at first but, my God, it doesn't take long to suddenly become aware of it and to become aware of things like unconscious bias.*

The interview further reinforced the fact that racism exists in all sectors of society and between different ethnic groups. However, few people talk about such things unless they are being affected in some way. In general, people feel uncomfortable and struggle to find the words, fearing that they may say the wrong things. Sometimes it can seem as if we, as individuals, inhabit different worlds or realities from those who are at the receiving end of racism and complain about it, and those who have the power or privilege of being blissfully unaware or cunningly denying its existence.

It's like a needle stuck on a particular track of a record, playing over and over. Then, every now and then, there's a slight shift, a small turn of the diversity wheel that offers a glimmer of hope for the marginalised groups; a glimmer of hope for us all, really – for humanity. Yet often, for so many of us, the changes are so small it seems as if nothing really changes. What we need is a paradigm shift – propelled by new conversations, new support and new challenges.

One of these small shifts occurred following the death of George Floyd, when individuals and organisations were galvanised into action. Unfortunately, the UK Government's recent report on racial and ethnic disparities may have set us several steps back, with its denials of racism in the country and its attempts to place blame on the victims of racism. This is evidence of politics and strategic racism in operation, and regrettably we all stand to suffer as the denials and disunity continues.

Empathy, compassion and fearing for the lives of others

I remember when I first heard about the death of US police officer, Brian Sicknick. I had watched the television footage as he and other officers battled to maintain control of protesters during the invasion of Capitol Hill. Another officer caught my attention – a black officer called Eugene Goodman, who was also trying to hold off the mob and was clearly terrified. At times, he was outnumbered by protesters and ran away; at other times, he stood his ground. I watched with my heart in my mouth, feeling enormous empathy for him and wondering why he was on his own. Being a black woman, I didn't find it difficult to empathise with him or understand the terror he must have felt as he stood face-to-face with mostly right-wing extremists who are widely known for their intolerance of racial differences.

It reminded me of the US serial drama, *Roots* (based on the book by Alex Haley, 1976), which I watched when I was very young; scenes of black people being chased, trapped and lynched. I still have nightmares about it. We often talk about post-traumatic stress disorder (PTSD) and psychological trauma, and can imagine the trauma the police officers must have experienced that day. Black or white, they were just carrying out their duty and were attacked in the process. Unfortunately, many black and ethnic minority employees experience psychological trauma as a result of the discrimination and racism they experience in the workplace. When they raise their concerns about racism, the standard response of organisations is one of denial and victim blaming. The silence and lack of support from their colleagues leave them feeling isolated and unsupported, further adding to their trauma.

Empathy seems to flow more freely when we are faced with someone who looks like us – that is, of the same colour, gender and so on. Writing about unconscious bias, Agarwal (2020) explained the importance of developing empathy. She described one study that shows how nurses were asked to imagine how much pain a patient was in and overcame their biases and prescribed adequate pain relief.

> *Todd et al.'s studies (2011) show the concrete social benefits of putting oneself in another person's shoes and that this can reduce unconscious bias and improve interactions between black and white people. Perspective-taking conditions showed a greater reduction in unconscious bias than participants who were asked to be objective. Dixon (2011), discussing this study, explains that we can keep our prejudices in check by putting ourselves in someone's shoes and trying to see the world through their eyes.*

However, as I said in #drshunguconversationsonrace (M'gadzah, 2021), we need to be aware of the dangers of only offering unconscious-bias training as part of an organisation's anti-racism strategy. Such training should be the starting point – we need to go 'beyond unconscious bias' (M'gadzah, 2021) and provide tools and strategies for individuals and organisations to better understand and deal with racism. Reflecting further on the interview of Prince Harry and Meghan Markle – and the responses that followed – the lack of interest and disregard for those who are not the same as 'us' is concerning. There are some people who find it difficult to have empathy or compassion for those who are racially different, and struggle to empathise with the Duchess. As Prince Harry said:

> *It takes living in her shoes for a day – for eight days – to see what she was going through and how far they (the press) were going to take it and get away with it and how blatant they were. I decided I've got to do something for my wife and for Archie as well because I could see where this was headed and where this was going to end.*

The couple said that they were never shown any public or private family support at Buckingham Palace.

> *What really upset me is that over 70 female members of parliament (Conservatives and Labour) came out and called out the colonial undertones of articles and headlines*

written about Meghan. But no one from my family said anything in the three years, and that really hurts.

Many of us who have experienced racism in the workplace will recognise the deafening silence and lack of support from colleagues, even colleagues who are close to us, who we consider to be our friends. Racism has the effect of polarising people. And being at the receiving end of racism this has the added effect of isolating victims. This reminds me of something Dr Martin Luther King said:

You will never forget the words of your enemies but you'll remember the silence of your friends.

The *Six Stages Framework* reminds us of the importance of showing compassion and empathy, even if someone is a different colour or looks different from us. Whether we like someone or not, we should be able to listen to them and show them compassion, especially (as in the case of Meghan Markle) if they tell you they are suffering from health issues and have suicidal ideation. Similarly, we should show compassion to those who tell us they are suffering from racial discrimination, whether it is conscious or unconscious. Sometimes it seems we 'switch off' such feelings for others, simply because they don't look like us, or because we don't like them.

We need to be brave enough to listen and observe what is going on within our organisation or community. Do we come to view them as less than human? The truth is that through our lack of tolerance and our inability to empathise or show compassion for those who are different, it is *us* who become less human. As I have written before (M'gadzah, 2020):

Without empathy and compassion, we are nothing but animals.

The most recent UK Government report on racial and ethnic disparities seemed to be devoid of empathy and compassion for black and ethnic minority groups. Chris Hemmings, the author of *Be a Man and How Macho Culture Damages Us and How to Escape It* (published in 2017), specialises in masculinity and empathy. In his book, he explained how masculine determination to be dominant not only impacts the women and girls in our lives, but also the men and boys. On the BBC News in March 2021 he talked about the disappearance and murder of Sarah Everard, and about collective social responsibility. As he explained:

... the media will usually frame the news is if it's a woman's responsibility to solve the problem. However we need to reframe our language in the reporting of these issues and not talk about women and safety issues, but rather about the violence of men against women and we need to get more men involved in the conversations.

He made reference to Martin Luther King's famous words, and stated:

We need men now to start speaking up, it's not about in a few days because this will not change unless men speak up. We have to get men involved in this and we need men to start speaking up right now – it's not about in a few days or in a few weeks, right now.

He also talked about the importance of instilling empathy into young boys and shifting the responsibility from women to men. He reflected on how to help boys and men realise what the consequences of their behaviours might be and the impact they may have on society as a whole. He talked about what's at stake if this work is not done.

Jackson Katz, PhD, is an educator, author and social theorist who is internationally renowned for his pioneering scholarship and activism on gender, race and violence issues. He works to promote gender equality and prevent gender violence, and is a co-founder of Mentors in Violence Prevention (MVP), one of the longest-running and most widely influential gender-violence prevention programmes in North America. Speaking on CNN in 2021, he talked about shaping the narrative and men taking the responsibility in this area:

> *Men will say 'I don't rape women and I don't abuse my girlfriend and my wife and so it's not my issue'. That's as ignorant as saying 'I'm a white person who doesn't burn crosses on my lawn and therefore racism is not my problem'. We are in the 21st century and we have accumulated knowledge of human-rights law and practice. And it's time we put that into practice and act on these basic sentiments. There are lots of conversations that we need to have together, whether it's about racism, gender issues or transgender.*

Basically, Katz reinforces the need for men to step up and take responsibility, in the same way that white people (and others) must step up and take responsibility for racism. We cannot keep turning away from these issues and treat them like they do not concern us. Similarly, the UK Government cannot blame ethnic minority people for their experiences and perceptions of racism. They cannot dismiss racism by suggesting that those who suffer from it are sensitised to discrimination, and that they should be more self-reliant and resilient.

The *Six Stages Framework* advocates for the need to have conversations together and change the culture around issues of race. Unless we start having real, honest conversations about racism in all its forms, in all sectors of society including schools, homes and our workplaces – and within the UK Government and the Royal family - we won't be able to change attitudes, cultures and behaviours where it is most needed.

Racism is not just a white–black issue

When preparing to engage with work on racial equity and inclusion, an important first step is to appreciate that racism is not just a white–black issue. It is also important to understand the definition of racism, and that racism is about power, and occurs when collective prejudice is backed by institutional control. As such, many will rightly state that black people cannot be racist because they do not have systemic power or control. The *Minnesota Daily* stated in 2020:

> *Any group of people can experience racial prejudice or discrimination. However, racism refers to that prejudice in addition to the socialized power structures at play.*

So, not everyone can experience the racism that Black people do, because the power dynamic that has existed since the Atlantic Slave Trade is just not equivalent to any other racial experience in the States.

The *Six Stages Framework* recognises the definitions of racism but also asserts that we need to expand our thinking around racism if we are to achieve real change. It is important that we focus first and foremost on values, attitudes and prejudice and the interplay of these factors between different groups. We need to accept and recognise that biases and prejudice exist in all racial groups. It's important to acknowledge this, and explore how it manifests and the impact it has.

Furthermore, work needs to be done to support all of us (black, white, Asian or other) to evaluate our biases and tackle institutional racism. It is only by making space for honest conversations around the re-evaluation of prejudice and biases within all groups that meaningful conversations around power and institutional racism can truly occur, without judgement or denial. The *Six Stages Framework* is based on this premise and applies a definition of racism that focuses on biases, attitudes, prejudice and discrimination and the belief that race is a determinant of traits and characteristics.

As mentioned above, racism occurs within all ethnic groups. The key components are fear of differences, blame of others, and power, which can all be present at different levels. It is true that we can all experience negative automatic thoughts, and can be quick to judge others – especially those who are different. It is also true that, just because people who differ from us are 'the same' within their own 'groups' (e.g. people of the same colour), they don't necessarily share the same values or accept one another; they can still be 'different'.

Biases and stereotypes also arise *within* the same ethnic groups and *between* cultural groups. I have been working with a group of people in Bangladesh, some of whom report discrimination based on within-culture differences and the caste system. This can be explained by a natural tendency to gravitate towards 'sameness' and to reject 'otherness' – a trait that is universal. The recent UK Government report (2021) refers to this as 'affinity bias'.

In her 2020 article on South-Asian prejudice and Asian anti-black racism, Alibhai-Brown referred to "inter-ethnic relations and inherited bigotries". She stated that Asians need to talk about the covert racism in their own communities, and described how other Asians are speaking out and:

... challenging elders and the normalized disparagement of discrimination against black people – as well as Asians with darker skin. ... How can we talk about Black Lives Matter when we are guilty of normalizing those attitudes in our countries and communities? You can't suddenly become an anti-racist because it is convenient.

She described how *Kaur Life*, a Sikh website, responded to Black Lives Matter:

... by running a brave series of articles, exposing the colourism, shadeism and anti-black attitudes that are sadly prevalent among South Asians.

She talked about the caste system, and the work of Professor Sunil Bhatia, a professor of human development at Connecticut College in the US who wrote about entrenched colour-coded and internalised colourism and xenophobia.

> *There is a line, [Bhatia] explains, that goes from in-group prejudices against members who are not fair-skinned, to racist recoil from people of African heritage.*

Alibhai-Brown called out the 'bigotry' within the Indian caste system, saying that it:

> *... is rooted in the Indian caste system which stipulates that fair-skinned castes are at the top of the social hierarchy and those of darker hues are at the bottom. Colonialism reinforced this supremacist ideology and, today, Bollywood carries on promoting the idea that fair is beautiful and dark is accursed. ... If we are honest, most Asian parents would probably object to their offspring marrying Africans or Afro–Caribbeans – and offer a host of excuses and prejudices to explain why.*

This is not the first time such issues have been raised. Alibhai-Brown wrote about Darshna Soni, the home affairs correspondent for Channel 4 News, who married her Ghanaian husband, Chi, almost twenty years ago. One of her relatives, whose husband is white, explained that she had 'married up' while Darshna, who had married a black man, had 'married down'. Alibhai-Brown stated in her article that Barnie Choudary (a former BBC correspondent) once said:

> *I was once asked whether I'd allow my daughter to marry someone who was African or Caribbean. Our children are going to fall in love and marry whomever they like. Why would you stop them? Our job, surely, is to empower them and give them the tools to stand up to, tackle and defeat racism.*

In her article, Alibhai-Brown also warned of the dangers of disunity amongst ethnic minority groups. Many black and Asian people do not accept the term BAME (which stands for 'black and Asian minority ethnic groups'), because their experiences and issues are so different and, as Alibhai-Brown stated, because the term 'disregards these realities'. Some people argue against increased representation as a solution to diversity, equity and inclusion; they prefer to focus on values-based leadership. These comments stem from private conversations with Umesh Prahbu in 2020–21, who worked as a medical director of two acute trusts for the NHS for fifteen years, focusing on patient safety, professional regulation, equality and diversity and leadership. He can be contacted on Twitter (@ drumeshprabhu).

The *Six Stages Framework* reminds us that we are all (white, black, Asian or other) at some point on a journey, either towards fully understanding and dealing with racial inequity and racism (thus promoting a more equitable society that does not discriminate between groups or individuals), or towards the rejection of differences and denial of equity and inclusion.

We must be aware that racism exists in all racial groups – that this work is not just for white people. We must all explore our biases and prejudices and question the areas of entitlement that have placed us in our various 'caves of privilege' – whatever those may look like.

We need to start having honest conversations about the differences that exist within ethnic minority groups. We are *not* all the same and we need to understand what makes us different and what divides us.

The rise in Asian hate crime and racism

Recently, we have seen the hate, animosity and violence directed at the Asian community as evidenced by the Atlanta Spa shootings in the USA, in which eight people, including six Asians, were shot. Asian protesters took to the streets to denounce the violence and racism directed towards them. Many Asian people are speaking up about how it feels to have racism directed their way. Here are some of the comments heard on CNN News:

> *"I feel so sick of being discriminated against; it reminds me of back at school when I got bullied in the whole kind of Asian fever I couldn't bear to be in my skin."*
>
> *"It's a terrible time to be Asian."*
>
> *"You hear about black people having the talk with their children, well right now in the Asian community we don't have such a thing and we don't really have the language to talk to children about what's happening to us. It reminds me of the fear I felt when I was younger hiding in my parents shop knowing that someone could just want to hurt me because of my colour."*

In 2021, Kyung Lah, a Korean–American journalist and correspondent, said on CNN News:

> *The assumption that people have about someone who looks like me, firstly that you don't speak English or that you may not understand everything they are saying. They always want to know where I'm from. It is a repeated question. The way you're treated is that you're not fully American. Assumption is that somehow you are foreign. Men prey to sexualise you who don't even know you. All of this is part of daily life and it has certainly got worse in the past year, because people are frustrated and they have to have a villain and vilify people. Almost as if saying you don't matter as much because you simply couldn't understand what we feel because of the way you look. ... If you've grown up in a bilingual family, the week of the shooting felt like being transported back into childhood, afraid that someone might hurt you simply because of the way you look – a deep-seated childhood fear that I carried for years and again during this week. Asian parents don't really have the language to explain how it feels to be foreign in your own home, and how it is to feel afraid without acting afraid or living afraid. It was a part of the programme at school and it was a part of class that day because there are so many children who need to have a way to cope with this and we don't currently have the language for this.*

It is clear from the events around the world that incidents of racial hate crimes (such as Asian hate crime, islamophobia and antisemitism) and victim blaming are increasing.

It happens everywhere and can affect all marginalised groups. Racism still exists in organisations, including the police force. Sadly, race prosecutions are at an all-time low. The *Six Stages Framework* is designed for individuals to explore these issues openly, in all racial groups, in all professional and community groups, and at all levels of society including schools.

The rise in violence against LGBTQ+ members and reframing the term 'coming out of the closet'

In June 2021, I heard Wade Davis (LGBTQ+ consultant and former NFL player) speaking on the BBC News about the Raider's lineman, Carl Nassib – the first openly gay NFL player. He had recently 'come out'. Davis reframed the expression 'coming out of the closet', which is used commonly by members of the LGBTQ+ community; he explained that:

> *It's not gay people coming out of the closet. It's more that they are inviting people into their world and trusting the world.*

He continued:

> *He's offering us an invitation to get to know him better; we don't come out of the closet; we're not monsters; we're not smelly shoes; we're not wire hangers. ... We are giving folks an opportunity to do better. ... It's actually society at large that is unsafe, that doesn't allow us to live in our humanity, so we are giving folks an opportunity to do better and to get better and therefore we will invite you in. It's also reframing the labour that we have to do. It's not LGBTQ folks that aren't present or visible. The work has to be done by the rest of society, not by the LGBTQ folk. ... We have always been here to be seen, it's just that we haven't trusted society at large to trust that they have the type of environment that allows us to live the way we want to in our humanity. The work is not for LGBTQ people to do; the work is for the rest of the world today. Steps that need to be taken to increase safety for LGBTQ.*

Nassib posted a video on Twitter about creating a culture that includes representation and visibility – that is accepting and compassionate. He spoke about the need to support LGBTQ+ youth and work on suicide prevention for this demographic. According to Amit Paley, CEO and executive director of the Trevor project:

> *Representation really does matter and Carl so openly in his truth will send a message to the young people that you can be who you want to be. People need to create a safe and accepting space for LGBTQ people.*

It is clear that we need to stop the attacks against LGBTQ+ and transgender people. We need to increase safety for them. But this can only happen when we create communities in which every person is valued, regardless of their differences – communities that allow individuals to embrace their identities without fear. We need to be able to support individuals and employees to manage and to nurture their identities in a modern world.

Understanding cultural differences and diversity

During my conversations on race (*#drshunguconversationsonrace*; M'gadzah, 2020), people opened up to me about their early experiences of 'difference'. It quickly became clear that we all had widely varying experiences that shaped us in very different ways. Some of the people I spoke to told me they didn't meet a black person until they were adults; others admitted they had never met a disabled or gay person. We rarely discuss such matters openly in our relationships or in the workplace; we are just expected to get on and work together, with no opportunity for exploring our humanity or our differences.

Sometimes we take our own experiences for granted and believe that everyone else has had the same amount of exposure to issues about racial difference and diversity. However, this is not the case. When I was working at The University of East London, a white student attended one of my tutorials, and told me I was the first black person she had 'been in a room alone with'. She was both excited and nervous – because she had never been 'exposed' to black people before.

When I mentioned this recently, a colleague of mine, who is white and Jewish, shared a similar experience. As a child, she heard her parents talking about black people but she never met one until she was in her twenties. Now she spends her time delivering diversity and inclusion training. I asked her when her particular services were called upon, and she explained that people usually approach her when they want to know what to do when they meet a black person for the first time.

This demonstrates my point. Although most of our experiences may not be so extreme, we cannot assume in our work or other interactions that other people have had the same level of 'exposure' as us to issues of diversity and racial differences. Some people have never met someone from a black and ethnic minority group, and others only socialise in ethnocentric groups (e.g. white-only, black-only or Asian-only groups). This makes the challenges for understanding, talking and dealing with issues of race even more complex. It can also throw up tensions in the workplace which are not fully understood or identifiable as being related to racial differences.

I know of a school in which there is a high proportion of Asian students from overseas. However, there is limited social interaction between them and the non-Asian students; they have very separate friendship groups. The school seems to accept this 'segregation', and the students resign themselves to the belief that this is 'just how things are'. Such a lack of social integration in some schools is a real concern because it often reinforces and perpetuates racial divides and stereotypes, and creates intolerances of differences and a 'them-vs-us' mentality. It would help to introduce the *Six Stages Framework* into the curriculum, to support teachers, children and young people to talk about differences and racism.

Owning and acknowledging our own biases and stereotypes

We all have automatic negative thoughts (Hollon and Kendall, 1980); they are perfectly natural. The issue is what we do about them when they arise. If they go unchallenged, they influence how we behave towards people who are different from us and can, unfortunately, turn into prejudice. A study by Iancu *et al.* (2015) found that people with higher levels of automatic negative thoughts were more likely to exhibit fear and avoidance. In #drshunguconversationsonrace, one of my colleagues told me how she is 'startled' when a black man walks behind her in a supermarket. Another colleague reported physically jumping when a black person opened the door as she entered it from the other side.

In the Oprah Winfrey interview with Meghan Markle and Prince Harry, Prince Harry mentioned an incident in which he had been asked 'how dark' their son Archie would be, because there were 'concerns' about the colour of his skin. Racism affects us all, and we cannot fully appreciate its impact until we speak to those who have experienced it first-hand. When people speak of their experiences and are 'brave' enough to share them with us, it is important to listen to them, and show compassion and empathy. (I use the term 'brave' here as it is not easy to share one's experiences, particularly in relation to such an emotive issue like racism.) It is often too easy to rush to a position of disbelief and not accept what someone is saying, or to dismiss their lived experiences as not being in line with reality (refer to the UK report on racial and ethnic disparities from March 2021).

After the interview with Meghan Markle and Prince Harry, Piers Morgan, co-presenter of ITV's *Good Morning Britain*, claimed Meghan Markle was lying about her mental health. However, the mental health charity MIND was quick to point out that we cannot disregard someone's experiences and comments about their mental health. Their website states:

> *We have seen encouraging and significant improvements in attitudes towards those of us experiencing mental health problems. Although we've made some great progress, we can't afford to lose momentum now; there is still much to be done when it comes to making sure that no one faces a mental health problem alone. Too often, feelings of shame and isolation mean people affected by mental health problems go without the help and support they need and deserve. Despite positive changes, we know when people do speak out, even today, too many people face discrimination across different areas of their lives – in the workplace, from family and friends, education, and from the health service.*

In response to Piers Morgan's comments, they posted on Twitter (@mindcharity):

> *We were disappointed and concerned to see Piers Morgan's comments on not believing Meghan's experiences about suicidal thoughts ... It's vital that when people reach out for support or share their experiences of ill mental health that they are treated with dignity, respect and empathy.*

Just as we should not be too quick to dismiss other peoples' mental health experiences, we should not be too quick to disbelieve or criticise peoples' lived experiences of racism. There have to be further improvements in attitudes in this area, and we need to make space for listening to these experiences. We should see the sharing of these experiences as an opportunity to learn and to engage in conversations, to make a real difference in our interactions with people who differ from us.

Understanding privilege and what it means

Privilege is when you think something is not a problem because it is not a problem to you personally.

This message appeared on a placard of an unidentified protester – a young white girl – in the video footage of the George Floyd protests on the BBC News in March 2021. It was previously referred to by @davidgaider in December 2014 as a quote from a colleague. In engaging with diversity, equity and inclusion work, it is important to understand the concepts of 'privilege' and 'entitlement'. In 2020, Amaechi wrote in an article about workplace diversity and equality, in which he said:

Privilege is not a pissing contest.

He elaborates on the subject:

Privilege is something we all understand even though we may argue that we don't have it. White privilege is often dismissed as a radical delusion or used to suggest people's lives are free of suffering – both are wrong. ... It is about understanding the hidden ways that different people's lives are made more difficult for reasons we often refuse to consider. No one privilege necessarily immunises a person from the challenges of the absence of another. Asking you to acknowledge your privilege does not minimise your personal hardship and suffering. It does not make your pain any less legitimate if you acknowledge someone else's pain which, by chance or birth, you find yourself free of. When it comes to white privilege, having it does not make your life easy but understanding it can make you realise why some people's lives are harder than they should be.

Concepts of privilege, and messages around 'uneven playing fields', have even reached fictional television characters. In November 2020, I listened to a character called Windass (portrayed by Mikey North) in the British soap opera *Coronation Street* talking to another character called Platt. They were speaking about Izzy Armstrong (played by Cherylee Houston) who is physically disabled and a wheelchair-user. The dialogue went like this:

***Windass**: You wouldn't think it to look at her, but Izzy lives in constant pain, a full-time job, great mum – you never hear her complain. You'd never know it to look at her.*

***Platt**: What shall I do? Give her a sash and crown?*

***Windass**: No. I'm just saying that she lives the hand that life dealt her.*

***Platt**: Yeah. We all do, don't we?*

> ***Windass**: I mean some of us start off with better hands than others, some of us lose hands along the way, but we all learn to play the hand that we are dealt.*

I shared his comments with some course participants and said, "Listen carefully. He is really talking about privilege in his own words!". The 2021 UK Commission report indicates a lack of understanding about privilege, which leads to a defensiveness. It is reflective of people at stages + 2, – 2 and – 3 of the *Six Stages Framework*, in that:

- They consider terms such as 'white privilege' to be highly controversial and alienating to those who do not feel especially privileged by their skin colour.
- They believe terms like 'white privilege' and 'white fragility' imply that "it is White people's attitudes and behaviours that primarily cause the disadvantage experienced by ethnic minorities".
- They believe that these terms "reinforce the perception that being an ethnic minority in the UK is to be treated unfairly by default".
- They prefer concepts and terms such as 'affinity bias' which they believe "usefully captures the tendency for groups to favour their own".

Understanding illusions and 'delusions' and how our beliefs shape our realities

Delusions are a symptom of many different psychiatric disorders. In clinical terms. They are considered to be psychotic disorders, in which the false beliefs are based on an incorrect interpretation of reality. In other words, people who are delusional have trouble recognising reality. According to Dunn and Bortolotti (2018):

> *Delusions are unusual beliefs that are held with conviction by the person who reports them, but appear implausible to a third party (American Psychiatric Association, DSM-5 2013, page 819). They can be poorly supported by evidence, resistant to counter-evidence, or inconsistent with other beliefs the person has. Clinical delusions can be symptoms of schizophrenia and dementia and might also be experienced by people with other mental health issues as well (such as amnesia and depression).*

It is recognised that 'clinically significant delusions' create anxiety and stress and impair good functioning, thereby leading to social isolation (Gunn and Bortolotti, 2018).

While delusions are viewed as 'maladaptive' responses that often ultimately cause distress, some have questioned whether delusions have a protective role (Gunn and Bortolotti, 2018; Roberts, 1992). There are those who believe that "delusions allow people to attribute meaning to their experiences" and have a defensive function in protecting the person from psychological distress (Roberts, 1992). In their article, Gunn and Bortolotti (2018) argued that:

> *The development of the delusional belief can play a short-term protective function. ... In the literature it has been suggested that some delusions can have an adaptive function by acting as defence mechanisms, protecting people from suffering or from*

unpleasant truths. Most of the cases discussed in the literature refer to psychological adaptiveness rather than biological adaptiveness. That is, the claim is that, at the time when they are adopted, some delusional beliefs make the person feel better about a certain situation, temporarily reducing anxiety or stress. Most of the evidence for the psychological adaptiveness of delusions is found in the discussion of so-called 'motivated delusions'. ... In the literature we briefly reviewed here, there is no attempt to deny the pervasive harmfulness of delusions. But, in different contexts and for different reasons, authors highlight the possibility that delusions might sometimes be adaptive, especially psychologically adaptive.

Recently, the term 'delusion' has appeared in a number of popular books and is increasingly used by psychologists and lay people to criticise those whose beliefs they do not agree with. Some have even suggested that people who complain about racism are deluded. In March 2021, John Amaechi, a psychologist and former professional basketball player, tweeted:

Have scanned the report on 'Black people, racism & human rights.' Stat after stat on inequalities in criminal justice, not explained by 'education'. Majority of Black people do not think treatment equal in healthcare or CJ. Conclusion feels like 'Black people are delusional'.

In his 2020 article, he also stated that:

... white privilege is often dismissed as a radical delusion used to suggest people's lives are free from suffering – both are wrong.

A recent UK Parliamentary enquiry report on the inequalities faced by many white children from working-class backgrounds suggested that many of them are 'achieving' worse than those from ethnic minority backgrounds (House of Commons, Education Committee, 2021). Many critics (such as Hood, 2021) have condemned the report, describing it as an:

... attempt to stoke the culture war.

And it was in danger of:

... legitimising narratives which are quite dangerous around white supremacy.

In an article published in June 2021, Hood stated:

In doing so, the report missed opportunities to show how the phrase could be used to reduce inequality. In fact, the concept of white privilege can and has been used to teach about other forms of privilege, including gender, class, sexuality, age, nationality and physical ability, to name a few. ... Rather than suggesting that white people face no challenges, white privilege highlights how a group of people are (and can be) affected by discrimination and disadvantage. It takes account of people's overlapping identities and experiences in order to understand the complexity of prejudices they face. This is also referred to as 'intersectionality'.

Similarly, others have accused some of former-US President Trump's supporters of being delusional (Linly, 2016). Kristof (2016) reflected on the attitudes of white Americans – about white beliefs with respect to black children's educational outcomes and their chances of getting a job – as delusional. He also referred to evidence of black delusions:

> *In fairness, the evidence shows black delusions, too. But what is striking in looking back at historical data is that blacks didn't exaggerate discrimination but downplayed it. … My hunch is that we will likewise look back and conclude that today's calls for racial justice, if anything, understates the problem – and that white America, however well meaning, is astonishingly oblivious to pervasive inequity. … We have tools that can help, although, of course, racial inequity is complex, involving not just discrimination but also jobs, education, family structure and more. A starting point is for us whites to wake from our ongoing mass delusions, to recognise that in practice black lives have not mattered as much as white lives, and that this is an affront to values that we all profess to believe in.*

In the following pages, I explore the use of terms like 'reality' and 'delusions' and draw upon some recent news reports about them. Delusions are defined as being adaptive and helpful, by not presenting reality. This is in contrast to the clinical definition of 'delusion' as mentioned above, and how it is understood. The term 'delusion' might be appealing, given its popularity these days, but I wonder whether it might be more useful to refer to a 'perception' based on experience, and suggest the word 'delusion' should be used with caution. We also need to be careful not to pathologise people's experiences – particularly in relation to those who report experiences of differences, including racism.

Fact, fiction, reality, illusion or delusion?

Recently, there has been an emphasis on the importance of 'facts' – as opposed to fiction – with concerns that the internet has seen the proliferation of so-called 'false news', whereby social media is a vehicle that transports and perpetuates falsehoods. At the same time, politicians are increasingly using 'fake news' to influence public opinion, with terms like 'spinning', 'audience shaping' and 'strategic racism' coming to the fore. The UK Commission report has suggested that people's experiences of racism are not real but based in the past. It's no wonder we are often left wondering what is true and what is not true. Scammers and politicians alike have taken advantage of this new technological world as they work to deceive us into believing the lies they weave and sell. Darren Lewis (2021) stated that the authors of the report only succeeded in *one* thing:

> *… showing themselves to be frighteningly detached from reality. … As exercises in delusion go, this report is right up there. … Today's landmark race review will embolden those who want to tell black and Asian people to 'get over it' and the report authors exhibit fantasy, delusion, and confused thinking.*

Early in 2021, I heard Derek Delgaudio, the author of *Amoralman: : A True Story and Other Lies* (2021), speak about morality, reality and illusions, and accepting 'the truth' – about truth and lies being two sides of the same coin. In his book, he questioned his own sense of morality and described the art of deception, and how, in our lives, we can find ourselves trapped inside an illusion. He explored the lies we tell ourselves and the realities we create around us, living out our fictions as if they were truths, stating:

> *People may not care about the truth or they might set up their value system so that it is difficult for them to accept it.*

He made reference to simulated poker games, and how realistic they feel to players, even though they are not real. He discussed his childhood, growing up with a mother who was gay and spending lots of time alone:

> *... this forced me into a sort of closet of my own. I grew up not wanting to be judged and therefore I spent time alone. One of the things you learn as a journalist is that you may never know what is true and if you do people may not care.*

He explained that even if people do care, their values and belief systems might not be set up to accept or believe the truth – it may be too painful for them to accept, and may reveal that their understanding of life is not true. No one wants to be made a fool or feel embarrassed. Some truths are simply too painful or uncomfortable to accept. As Delgaudio stated:

> *I don't think we really have real conversations about seeing one another. I think most of the conversations that are had these days are either political or politicised, other than maybe in a self-help context.*

He also described his astonishing theatre show and movie, *In And Of Itself* (Hulu, 2021), as a Trojan horse for that same conversation – the human conversation:

> *I wanted people to see what it's like to be in this world and to be connected in a way that we are and the real consequences attached to that – 'How I see you matters'. ... human conversation about what it is to see one another and to be in this world and to be connected in a way that we can't ignore in that we are all shaping each other's identities and that there is real consequences attached to that, but how I see you matters and how I see you and recognise you or if I choose to deny you then that matters. ... We are all the unreliable narrators of each other's stories but I'm not just defined by what you see, I am also defined by all the things you will never see.*

The show uses magic to illustrate points about personal identity and what is real and what is not. It reminds us of our common humanity by breaking through what we see, demonstrating that whatever is presented to us is not necessarily the truth.

> *Magic and illusion are used as a metaphor about identity and what we can and cannot see about each other.*

Delgaudio described how people have real transformations when they watch it, and how it makes them consider their identities, the way they see themselves and the way they wish others to see them; it forces people to say who they are. As he explains:

> *I remember reading that true identity is one which exists within one's own heart and is seen by another. ... We realise that these labels we give ourselves and that we give each other are the limitations that we have.*

In his book, he explored how much people are willing to believe untruths – because they want to believe them – and that they are "scary on all levels, including politically". He observed:

> *How easy it is to live in a fiction that's written by others and living it as if that it was true, particular when it comes to democracy and voting. It becomes less about truth and more about humanity for me.*

He also raised some important existential questions around 'How I see you matters', pertinent to racism. He addressed others too:

> *Do I see you as you really are, or how I choose to see you? ... as someone who is a threat to my existence and who is not equal to me?*

Recently in politics, on social media and in relation to the Covid-19 pandemic, we have seen people make decisions based less on the truth and more on what they want to believe. We have to be reminded that facts matter. An advert on CNN said: "This is an apple not a banana. Some people might try to tell you it's a banana".

The storming of the Capitol in the US occurred because some people were persuaded (some even say they were groomed) to believe that America is only for certain types of Americans – those who look the same as those who are white – and that ethnic minorities are a threat to a 'greater America' because they take away jobs and homes.

When we actively work to exclude others, and see them as a threat to our very existence, it forces them to hide their true identities. People will hide who they are as they do not feel safe enough to share their true identities with society. As Amaechi once said in relation to gay people 'coming out of the closet', people think that when someone 'comes out' they are telling you something about them – but they're not; they are telling you something about you. They're saying:

> *I think you'll be able to hear this – not judge me, but treat me with respect.*

Amaechi (2017) explained it like this:

> *They're basically saying I'm entrusting you with my identity and that you will treat my identity with the very same care that I do.*

The *Six Stages Framework* reminds us that racial equity is truly about humanity and how we see and interact with each other on a human level, without interference from politics or entitlement or the caves of privilege we inhabit. The challenge we have is to remember and to show that we are all humans, and we can do this by showing empathy and compassion. Positive progression along the six stages goes from + 1 to + 6, however it is worth noting that the stages can also go the *opposite* way, in a negative direction from – 1 to – 6. The negative trajectory indicates what can happen when falsehoods are perpetuated and people look for someone or something else to blame. Their views become more entrenched, and open to radicalisation, potentially resulting in more extremist beliefs, behaviours and even violence (see Fig. 1). This is what we saw with the Capitol riots.

While the world is becoming more sensitive to racial issues because of Black Lives Matter, some people (including politicians) exploit people's fears of difference and use racist ideas for their own benefit. Unfortunately, there are people out there who are desperate enough to believe them. While many would argue that the Capitol riots were a reaction to the election being 'stolen' by Democrat fraud – that they were not overtly about racism – others have questioned the role that racism played in them (Black, 2021; *New York Times*, 2021).

The UK Commission report on race and ethnic disparities addressed perceptions and realities of racism. It stated that overt and outright racism exists and persists within the UK, and that it looms large in our minds due to social media and visibility of such things as graffiti on walls. It also suggested that the experiences of some people on social media amplify perceptions of racism and shape their realities, and that racism is made worse by the prevalence and visibility of racism online.

> *The gravitational forces of dominant narratives tends to point our attention in negative directions such as racist abuse on social media and away from positive ones, the fact, for example, that 40% of NHS consultants are from ethnic minorities. ... Also, if it were true that Black and South Asian groups were suffering from systemic racism throughout their lives – adversely affecting their health, education, income, housing, employment (the key determinants of health) – this would be reflected in overall mortality figures across the life-course. ... And they tend to stress the 'lived experience' of the groups they seek to protect with less emphasis on objective data. It is not surprising therefore that mainstream public debate about race sensitises minorities to discrimination, but does less to highlight minority self-reliance and resilience.*

The Commission report sought to redefine institutional racism:

> *... we have argued for the use of the term 'institutional racism' to be applied only when deep-seated racism can be proven on a systemic level and not be used as a general catch-all phrase for any microaggression, witting or unwitting.*

It almost seems the authors of the report are suggesting that microaggressions are not racism; however, I would argue that there is a need to understand the different 'shades' of racism, which I refer to later in this book. The report attempted to shift away from the well-known Macpherson definition of racism used in the Stephen Lawrence inquiry. Lawrence was a black British teenager, murdered in a racially motivated attack while he waited for a bus in 1993. In the inquiry, the UK police were found to be institutionally racist, defined as:

> *The collective failure of an organisation to provide an appropriate and professional service to people because of their colour, culture, or ethnic origin. It can be seen or detected in processes, attitudes and behaviour which amount to discrimination through unwitting prejudice, ignorance, thoughtlessness and racist stereotyping which disadvantage minority ethnic people.*

Instead, the UK Government's Commission focuses on individual factors and social class as reasons for inequality and denies racism as a factor. The UK Government is well aware of how difficult it is to prove racism on any level – let alone what they call 'deep-seated racism' at a systemic level (whatever that means).

We know some organisations go to extreme lengths to hide the realities of racism within their walls, distorting evidence and discrediting those who bring such claims. I have described the government as being disingenuous (M'gadzah, 2021), and others on social media have described it as attempting to gaslight the public.

Working to adapt to the world —is there such a thing as 'useful delusions'?

Shankar Vedantam wrote in his 2021 book, *Useful Delusions: The Power and Paradox of the Self-Deceiving Brain*, that we need to consider some of the 'delusions' we have on top of our beliefs.

> *Our brains are designed to operate to mediate between the outside world and the inside world. And this is not by presenting reality in its complete accuracy but in presenting delusions that might help us and how we operate. I believe that our brains are actually constantly coming up with theories and models of the world. And when you look at signs of delusions, it's not actually just a case of brainwashing but that the brain is mediating between the outside world and the inside world. And one of the ways that the brain mediates is by not presenting reality in its complete accuracy to us, but in coming up with solutions that may actually help us adapt and be more functional in the world. Parents start teaching their children this and this begins almost before we open our eyes. Delusions are not a sign of brainwashing. We come up with solutions that might actually help us adjust and adapt to the world.*

He explained that delusions occur at high and low levels, with 'lower-end' delusions being the beliefs we have, such as: "all of our own ethnic group is good and other groups are not" or "our parents love us". He also said:

> *Our brains filter out information to stop us from becoming overwhelmed. So they present us with information we can take advantage off and act on, reflecting on what has been useful to us in the past. This is the role that the brain plays all the time. Often the brain does this in a way that is helpful but there are times when it can do it in unhelpful ways.*

He went on to describe the idea of our brains having 'ambassadors' who filter the information we are presented with:

> *Our brains are designed to pay attention to threats but also to manage them in a way that is helpful. Sometimes we create these delusional beliefs to help us cope and to manage. Our brains filter out what we're able to tolerate, to enable us to see the world in more delusional ways so that we survive and cope. Depressed people may actually be seeing the world more accurately.*

Could it be possible that we come up with 'delusions' that we think will keep us safe in our realities and deep within our caves? I was discussing Vedantam's book with a black colleague of mine who said:

> *I found this explanation of how we construct our reality fascinating. I believe I experienced a challenge to my reality and my perception when I was watching Noughts and Crosses by Malorie Blackman (2001). In my early childhood I'd been brought up attending mainly white schools and with only white friends. I build my life around this and was generally very happy as I managed the situation based on this reality. A friend of mine who knew me back then often says to me 'But you were happy during those times. Did you experience any racism? The truth is yes I was happy, and yes I did experience racism, but I found ways of filtering this out in order to preserve my sanity. When I watched Noughts and Crosses, I found myself feeling discomfort at such an intense level, almost as if I wanted to switch the roles back again to the reality I was used to – that of white people having the power and being in control. It reminds me of Stockholm syndrome where the abducted and abused end up wanting to protect their abuser.*

She went on to explain how she has learnt to cope and preserve her friendships:

> *I found ways of challenging my own 'perception' and addressing my experiences. I still have many white friends who are very dear to me but I also have black friends. I still find myself at times not challenging my white friends if they say something which is 'not quite right' in terms of race. I challenge some things, but choose not to challenge others, simply to preserve friendships. My view is that we need to choose when we make these challenges, as sometimes they will not be heard.*

In his book, Vedantam also stated:

> *We sometimes need to find ways of empathizing with people's delusions and not immediately challenging them.*

It could be said that my colleague found ways of navigating her own perceptions or 'delusions' about the reality she created when she was younger, as well as the 'delusions' of her friends in terms of the reality some of them are used to. In essence, she (and some of her friends) may be on the first (+ 1) or second (+ 2) stages of the *Six Stages Framework*. They are not bad people – they simply need to be supported to start the journey in understanding racism and dealing with issues of racial inequity and inclusion more fully. However, there will be others who are at stages – 1 and – 2, who make it clear that they are not interested in understanding racism and are on a negative trajectory. In the words of Prince Harry, each one of us must "do the work and their own learning"; but first – and most importantly in my opinion – we need to recognise the *need* for the work and they need to *want* to do it.

As Vedantam suggested in his quote above, our brains sift out what we're not able to tolerate so that we can deal with things like anxiety in ways that we can tolerate. People with mental illnesses can find this difficult, resulting in anxiety that may be overwhelming. However, some of them may actually see the world more accurately than those without a mental illness.

I believe many people respond to racial inequity and racism in the same way, sifting out information that fits with and supports their reality and perception. This explains some of the experiences people face through gaslighting – a form of psychological manipulation in which one person 'seeks to change another person's beliefs or perceptions and behaviours through indirect deceptive and underhand tactics' (Wikipedia). Victims find themselves questioning how someone can possibly think or believe such things. The truth is that gaslighters want others to think the same way as them, because that is the reality they have constructed for themselves – that is the cave they inhabit.

Can the same be said for people who complain about racism? Are they suffering from false belief systems? Are they 'deluded' and stuck in their own self-constructed realities? The people quoted above certainly force us to question what 'reality' is and what 'delusions' are. The UK Government report suggested that those who complain about racism are stuck in the past – that their perceptions are not in line with reality and that they have overly pessimistic narratives. Is this true? Could the experiences of so many be wrong? Or is the UK Government merely 'audience shaping'?

Questioning people's perceptions of reality is a form of gaslighting. It occurs in stages +2 and – 2 in the framework, and down to stage – 6. It is no wonder Amaechi (2021) said in response to the UK Commission report:

> *Black and brown people, you are not delusional. Your experiences are not a myth. Our experience is not a myth.*

A colleague of mine told me there is a real danger that all these reports and discussions serve to present a pathologising perspective of people's experiences of racism, and are designed to create confusion. She asked the following question:

> *If people of colour are explaining their reality to others, and their perception is understood or considered to be a delusion, it then becomes unclear who has the delusion – the people that complain of having been racially discriminated against or the people who deny racist behaviours when confronted?*

In a world where everyone is talking about delusions and questioning each other's realities, who exactly is 'deluded'? This is an important question and one that I explore further, in Chapter 12. This was also echoed in a comment I heard on Radio 4 in July 2021, by Alan Ayckbourn, the British playwright and director. He said:

> *If I had another play left in me it would be on this ... the internet these days, everyone has their own version of the truth. You don't quite know who to believe.*

Audience shaping—what we believe and why we believe it

It is clear that the UK Commission report is an attempt at 'audience shaping'. It certainly seems as though the authors may have manipulated the data and selected pieces of evidence that support their claims, while ignoring other data and evidence that do not. Worse still, it seems the report aims to make people question their realities and believe the one presented in the report which states that racism is a thing of the past despite evidence that proves otherwise. In a world of fake news and false narratives, we will be forced to work that much harder to hold onto our own realities. Lewis (2021) responded to claims in the UK Commission report, stating:

> *The only response is to continue providing the clear, statistical and anecdotal evidence to undermine the fantasy, delusion, and confused thinking.*

In June 2021, Aamna Modhin interviewed Samuel Kasumu about his reasons for quitting his role as the UK Prime Minister's minority adviser. She reported that Kasumu's warning that:

> *Exploiting division for electoral gain could spark another Stephen Lawrence or Jo Cox tragedy.*

I posted the following on LinkedIn in response to her article:

> *This article confirms all of my fears. I have almost completed my book Understanding and Dealing with Racism – The Six Stages. I warn of the dangers of divisive politics and the dire consequences. As I was writing my book I found myself thinking, maybe I am overreacting. This article confirms that this is not the case. Unfortunately many people don't realise the consequences of their actions and this includes politicians. We need to be careful about what we say and we need to avoid fuelling hatred or, as Samuel Kasumu points out, it's not okay to incite division: 'there are some people in the government who feel like the right way to win is to pick a fight on the culture war and exploit division. I worry about that and it seems like people have very short memories and they have already forgotten Jo Cox'. I totally agree with Kasumu's sentiments. The way I see it is that we all are on this planet together and we are all human beings first and foremost. What we say matters and it influences others, and we all need to wake up and realise this – and be alert to the dangers of sowing hatred. The consequences will outlive and affect us all.*

Leadership matters, and anyone in a leadership position needs to realise that others look to them for how they should behave; as such, their behaviours, words and actions are extremely important. This useful description from Vedantam clarifies what is meant by 'audience shaping':

> *All of us modulate what we say so that part of what we say appeals to the people we are speaking to. We try and present ourselves to be suitable to our listeners. ... As we do this, we start to believe what it is that we have just said, so the act of speaking actually creates its own belief structure. It is called 'audience tuning' so that as a politician speaks the audience is actually shaping what the politician is saying and as the politician speaks her words actually shape what she herself believes.*

He also explained that even when our beliefs don't 'come true', we sometimes come up with ways to rationalise them. This is cognitive dissonance, when our reality tells us one thing, and our inner world tells us otherwise. We find ways of seeing things in a new light and to create a new reality. Some say this is what is happening in the USA; some Republicans continue to believe that the US election was stolen from them, and that their President, Trump, will be back in the White House, despite clear evidence that he lost the election an example of seeing reality 'delusionally', to make it fit with our view.

Therefore, I ask again: how can the experiences of so many be so wrong? Vedantam pointed out that hundreds of people may share the same delusion, but we have to question what conditions allow such a delusion to flourish. He explained that all of us have an aversion to feeling out of control. When this happens, we are more likely to believe 'false truths' perpetuated by political leaders – for example, that their own population's suffering is caused by others, such as those who are racially different. Perhaps ex-President Trump's messages resonate with such people's 'delusions'.

Messages from the Black Lives Matter movement may be considered by some to resonate with black people's 'delusions'. At least, this appears to be what the UK Government report is suggesting, by pointing to the influence of social media on shaping realities. If people who experience racism can be described as 'deluded', surely the same logic can be applied to those who display racism. Are we heading into a future in which it is difficult to know what's real and what's fake, or who is and who isn't 'deluded'?

The UK has a government that tells its people that their experiences are not grounded in reality. We also have television presenters like Piers Morgan who not only questioned and rejected Meghan Markle's description of her own mental health, but also attempted 'audience shaping', for example by suggesting how cruel she and Prince Harry were to raise such issues during a difficult time for the Royal family (when the Duke of Edinburgh's health was failing).

So, where do we go from here? Clearly many people choose what they want to believe and attempt to summon up evidence to support their point of view and confirm their realities. Both sides of an argument could argue that the other is 'deluded'. This is happening with the Covid-19 pandemic vaccination programme, where there is real division in terms of what people believe and the sources of information they use to corroborate their respective positions.

The *Six Stages Framework* shows us that 'delusions' (and 'audience-shaping') occur on the negative axis, as false and faulty belief systems take hold and become increasingly entrenched. This happens to anyone, regardless of their colour, race or ethnic background; it also occurs regardless of power. Someone can be black, white, Asian or other and find themself on a downwards trajectory on the *Six Stages* negative axis, fuelled by intolerance and hatred for those from different ethnic and racial backgrounds.

However, it is misleading and manipulative to suggest 'delusions' occur for the majority of those who complain about racism – this is simply untrue; the majority of people who complain about racism are on the positive axis.

In the area of DEI, we see 'delusions' play out as faulty entrenched beliefs. Often those who harbour them become intent on blaming others, with no evidence or facts to support their claims. Their beliefs and behaviours become extreme, irrational and detached from reality, as occurs from stages −1 to −6; indeed, black and ethnic minorities can also find themselves on this path including, for example, those who falsely make claims of racism in the belief that everyone is racist, or those who deny racial differences and blame anyone who is racially different from them.

So how do we navigate this situation? How can we understand what is true and what is not, whose reality is real and whose isn't? Do we remain in our corners – the corners of our caves – confident that our own reality is the truth and that everyone else is deluded or lives in a make-believe world? Vedantam had this to say:

> *When we think about the delusions that affect all of us around the world, we need to think about ways of spreading opportunities more equitably. We need to remove the soil in which delusions can spread; that in itself might be the way to combat dangerous delusions – by providing more equitable conditions in society, for example, how to provide access to healthcare and education more equitably. ... When we think about people who have delusions we often look at them from outside of what they are experiencing. The ability to not engage in delusions can be seen as a form of privilege. That is, if your life is going great and your job is going great then you have no need to turn to beliefs and delusions because your life is fantastic. But in a moment when that's taken away from you, when you feel vulnerable and you feel scared and insecure, it turns out that all our minds very quickly gravitate to beliefs and delusions because those beliefs can soothe us from our greatest fears and anxieties.*

Vedantam also explained that sometimes we need to be okay with the 'delusions' of others, and not necessarily challenge them on the spot, in order to empathise with them; this can mean putting aside our rationalisations and logic to help them cope. Sometimes we may have to set aside 'the facts' and stop 'forcing' our beliefs or values onto others, and simply listen. We shouldn't try to persuade others of our viewpoints in the area of racism because this often leads to polarisation – whereby people become stuck and unwilling to shift from their perceived realities.

So how do we support those who find themselves on the negative axis? Do we ignore racism and people's experiences of it on the negative axis, and say they are 'deluded' and not in touch with reality? Do we accuse those complaining of racism on the positive axis of having overly pessimistic narratives? Should we ignore those who say that racism does not exist – that it is a radical illusion? Or should we ignore those who see black and ethnic minorities as a threat to their existence?

The simple answer is no. But we do need to spend more time engaging in conversations to try to understand the realities people live in, and how they are constructed, and we need to provide safe spaces for having conversations, for shining a light on these constructions and any so-called 'delusions' (including 'delusions' at a government level). At the same time, we should attempt to understand the role and purpose that these 'delusions' serve. It is rarely possible to remove them through persuasion or a one-off session on unconscious-bias training.

What is needed is a process of self-reflection, and conversations that seek to understand individual and organisational realities and how and why they have been constructed. We need new tools for a new age, because previous tools have not been shown to be as effective as they might (Hecht, 2020); tools such as the *Six Stages Framework*, which assesses individual and organisational biases, measures baselines and provide support for growth and improvement. We must all start doing our 'our own learning' (Prince Harry, 2021) and reflection as part of a process; we can refer to this as diversity 'therapy' or 'personal and organisational development'.

We should be able to measure the extent to which an organisation's culture is inclusive or biased – the extent to which managers and senior leaders understand and promote inclusion by carrying our DEI leadership evaluations. I believe that part of the 'measurement' has to be listening to the experiences of ethnic minorities who are on the positive axis (and the negative axis) within their community or organisation, and not dismissing them as being out of touch with reality or suggesting that they are hiding away from the progress that has been made.

We also need to listen to white people or anyone who finds themselves on the negative axis, engaging in honest and open conversations about the realities of racism, so we can all better understand how it manifests.

The historical contexts of countries steeped in racist and colonial pasts help us to understand the behaviours and beliefs of those in certain institutions, such as the UK government and the Royal family. While some might view this as a continued focus on overly pessimistic narratives, others stress how important it is for us to continue to educate ourselves about the past and learn from it, and understand how it continues to impact us in present times. This is not to say that we should keep living in the past, but rather that we can use lessons from the past to ensure that the mistakes of the past do not continue to harm people in the present. The portrayal of the Royals by Prince Harry and Meghan Markle – each of them living their lives and performing their jobs on the world stage, feeling like they're in a zoo, and of the Royal family's symbiotic relationship with the press – is an interesting one. It raises further questions about what's real and what's not, and gives us insight into the contractual relationship of the Royal family with the press – the former feeling trapped for fear of upsetting them.

Part of helping people cope with their reality and navigate their 'delusions' is to appeal to their humanity and help them understand how their interactions with others matter – to help them understand what it feels like to be in someone else's shoes, or to achieve a sense of belonging while supporting them to recognise others' need for belonging too. The Six Stages framework emphasises the importance of 'Managing and nurturing our identities in a modern World" (M'gadzah, 2021). We all have a role to play and need to consider how we influence and shape each others' identities.

This approach has to come from a place of genuine listening, curiosity and willingness to understand other people's experiences without judgement or blame. The UK Government places blame on the people who complain of racism, and this is not helpful; such a strategy will prevent the country from moving forwards and will, if anything, set us back from the progress we made after the deaths of Stephen Lawrence and George Floyd.

Concerns about racist attitudes in the Royal Family polarise the nation

Jane Martinson, a columnist for *The Guardian*, reported on the BBC News about the differential treatment of Meghan Markle and Kate Middleton (the Duchess of Cambridge) in the tabloid press, suggesting there is significant bigotry and racism.

The Society of Editors denied these claims, but were immediately criticised in a letter signed by one hundred and sixty-seven journalists of colour, and the editors of the *Financial Times* and *The Guardian*. It seems that from Harry and Meghan's perspective, the media had been inciting racism. Unfortunately, issues of race have the ability to create conflict and polarise nations, as happened in both the UK and US.

Whenever concerns or claims are made about racism, organisations tend to move immediately to a 'default programme', often denying the allegations. Sadly, this only makes things worse because it blocks further learning opportunities. Following the interview of the Sussexes, concerns were raised about racist attitudes and racism within the Royal family, about whether they are racist; however, many were quick to assert that they are not. Prince William, keen to restore reputational damage, responded to a journalist's direct question by stating, "We are very much not a racist family".

Regrettably, the situation isn't so simple: it is possible to not be at the extreme end of the racism spectrum, yet to have certain values, beliefs, attitudes and behaviours that involve the differential treatment of people who are racially different.

It is equally true that there are people who have done amazing work for charities, yet they are still intolerant of people of colour, such as the example Alibhai-Brown gave of black people marrying into Asian families (Alibhai-Brown, 2020) and the fictional character, Miss Millie, in *The Color Purple* (Walker, 1982).

By reflecting on what I have said about realities and 'delusions', it could be argued that the polarisation of the UK about the Royal family created a divide between those who support the Royal family and those who support Meghan and Harry, demonstrating the tendency of some people to cherry-pick what information they absorb, to maintain their own perceptions of their realities. It is going to be very difficult to change their views.

The Sussexes also criticised the British media for their racist undertones and incitement of racism. For some, it's as if someone can only be 'racist' if they show 'overt' racism. Unfortunately, the reality is far more nuanced than that, whereby people can fall anywhere on the prejudice–racism spectrum (Fig. 6 on page 92). As mentioned before, even the most dedicated charity worker can also be racially intolerant. Clearly these are not simple black-and-white issues – there are many shades of grey; and as Alibhai-Brown (2020) described, even members of black and ethnic minority communities can hold racist views.

Scales of racial intolerance and racism: Everyone has a responsibility to open up conversations

People at stages +1 and +2 of the *Six Stages Framework* would not be considered racists in the overt (direct) sense of racism. Matters of racial equity and inclusion are simply not on their radar, and they are not really interested. This inevitably impacts on their attitudes, behaviours and treatment of those who are racially different. Left unchallenged, these can turn into prejudices or more extreme forms of intolerance and racism.

When we consider issues of racism, it is important to reflect on our beliefs and the reasons for those beliefs. It is not right to simply brand someone a 'racist and then wave them goodbye! We have to stop polarising issues of race and going to extremes when we talk about racial equity, inclusion and racism. When issues are raised, many people block discussions, for example by saying "I'm not a racist", which prevents valuable conversations and learning.

Each of us has a shared responsibility to open up conversations and try and understand each other's values, beliefs, perceptions and realities. It is only by having such conversations that the possibility of change exists.

The lack of interest in or disregard for those who are not the same as us, as demonstrated recently by police in the USA and Belgium, is concerning. It can lead to a situation in which people find it difficult to have empathy or compassion for those who are racially different, and can lead to the treatment of others as 'less than human', with potentially devastating consequences, as in the case of George Floyd, and more recently in the UK (November 2021) in the case of two white police officers who shared Whatsap pictures of the murdered black sisters, Bibaa Henry and Nicole Smallman.

Several members of the backbench Common Sense Group of Tory MPs and peers criticised Barnado's Children's Charity for publishing a blogpost on its website discussing racial inequality and white privilege. The Charity Commission (the regulatory body of charities in England and Wales) rejected a complaint that accused Barnardo's of breaching its charitable purposes by publishing what they called an 'ideological dogma'. Butler, a social policy editor, published this in the Guardian:

> *The Barnardo's post, which remains on the charity's website, offers parents tips on how to discuss 'white privilege' with their children. It explains that the charity's white service users faced 'inequality and disadvantage' on a daily basis, but those from black and minority ethnic backgrounds face additional challenges due to their skin colour.*

The Charity Commission found that the Barnardo's blog was in line with the charity's mission, and that they had acted reasonably and within the law. No regulatory action was deemed necessary. Butler described the charity's reaction to the findings and its view on the role it has to play in supporting difficult conversations thus:

> *Barnardo's said it welcomed the decision: 'As the UK's largest children's charity, we believe we have a legitimate role to play in encouraging an informed approach to difficult conversations about complex issues, including racism. We have always spoken out on the challenges affecting the children we serve, and must continue to do so – whether on poverty, mental health, abuse and exploitation – or on the realities of prejudice and discrimination'.*

7

Coming out of 'caves of privilege'

Shades of racism and the prejudice–racism spectrum—time to call out casual racism

In 2018, Luvvie Ajayi, author and digital strategist, wrote about the need to call out casual racism, stating:

> *We can't have an honest reckoning about race until we start to recognize all the ways in which privilege and prejudice creep into our lives. ... Microaggressions and instances of casual racism like this pepper our daily lives, leaving a terrible taste in our collective mouths.*

She referred to some of the defensive responses described earlier that occur when we question displays of casual racism:

> *Some well-meaning folks think if we stop talking about racism it'll magically disappear.*

From reflecting on the interview of Prince Harry and Meghan Markle and other issues of racial equity and inclusion, it might appear, broadly speaking, that there are two types of people: racists and non-racists. But as I pointed out earlier, the situation is far more nuanced. We are all somewhere on a spectrum. This is probably true of the Royal family and the UK Government, as well as the rest of us.

There are numerous shades of racial intolerance, forming a spectrum, and underlining the importance of not polarising issues of race, or stopping discussions by saying 'I'm not racist'. Meghan Markle's father commented on Royal enquiries about Archie's skin colour by saying he didn't consider the Royals to be racist, but "someone may have just asked a dumb question". We have to understand that such 'dumb questions' may not appear to be an extreme form of racism, but they *are* on the spectrum because they indicate some biases, prejudices or microaggressions that involve discrimination, which will perpetuate if we fail to deal with them (Fig. 5). They point to some underlying or simmering prejudice that is at risk of bubbling over into more insidious and extreme forms of racism. In July 2021, I wrote in a post on LinkedIn, 'Racism is not a black or white issue', and posed a question:

> *What if we viewed prejudice and racism as a spectrum? People would say, 'we are all somewhere on the spectrum and we all have traits which show up as biases and prejudice'. If so, where would you be on that spectrum?*

In the context of the Six Stages Framework (Figs 1 and 2), people at stages +/– 1 and +/– 2 are 'not racists in the extreme sense of the word'. However, some of them are guilty of 'casual' racism, as defined previously, whereby issues of racial equity and inclusion are not on their radar – they are not interested or aware of the issues others face, or do not accept their experiences. Similarly, people at stages – 2 and – 3 (Fig. 1) are not radical or terrorists; however, their behaviours and beliefs show a level of 'intent', which makes them vulnerable to being groomed or radicalised. If they proceed further on the negative axis, that is more concerning and they may pose a real danger to those who are different (Figs 1 and 4). We all need to appreciate the damaging effects of *all* forms of racism on individual people and on society, regardless of position on the racism spectrum. Casual racism is still racism (Figs 5 and 6).

The 2021 UK Commission report seemed to criticise the changing conceptualisations and definitions of racism. These definitions need to change and evolve as we gain more understanding of how racism operates and of new terminology (e.g. microaggressions). In a paper by Etutu and Shearing (2021), Astrid Guillabeau (a French national) who lives with her partner, Mike Munyao (who has Kenyan and Rwandan heritage), had this response to the Harry and Meghan interview:

> *Hearing the claims is shocking but it's not shocking. Racism is out there. I have people touching my kids, touching their hair, touching their face – strangers. ... And ignorance is no excuse for racism.*

So it is time now for us to start opening up these conversations and support people to better understand racism, how it operates and how to deal with it. We must *move past* the point where people ask questions like: 'But is it racist if you ask how dark a child's skin colour will be?', or 'Is it racist to say that I don't see colour – everyone is the same to me'?, or 'Is it racist to touch a black child's hair?'.

I spoke earlier about 'caves of privilege'. What do we do about the caves that people so carefully construct as part of their realities over the years? How do we begin to dismantle them? And how does anyone begin to take steps to emerge from them?

The first step is to recognise where we are and how we got here. Acknowledging biases and privileges is a good starting point, as is talking about the lived experience of those who are different. Then it is possible to move past the stage of sharing and listening to others' lived experiences, and feeling guilty, ashamed, shocked or surprised by them.

We must take steps to deconstruct 'caves of privilege' wherever we find them. As a disabled white friend of mine recently told me, about the privilege of being able bodied:

> *Being chronically disabled now is totally different from imagining it and trying to walk in a disabled person's shoes in the past, and knowing plenty of people with disabilities and talking to them about their struggles! Lived experience is the only sure guarantee of truly understanding. Initiatives like the Six Stages Framework will take so many people further along that spectrum in terms of their ability to understand and deal*

Fig. 4: Spectrum of racism on the negative axis of the Six Stages Framework.

Racial intolerance and prejudice		Indirect racism	Increasing intolerance and direct racism		Leadership action
Exhibits indirect racism Exhibits biases and prejudice Thinks in and uses stereotypes Asks so-called 'dumb questions' Makes 'innocent' jokes about differences that undermine and act as put-downs	Exhibits indirect racism Exhibits biases and prejudices Thinks in and uses stereotypes Exhibits micro-aggressions Uses racial slurs and casual racist remarks Uses gaslighting	Exhibits direct and indirect racism Exhibits increasing intolerance When called out, excuses behaviour as 'just banter' Undermines those who are different (e.g. makes disparaging comments)	Exhibits direct and indirect racism Exhibits microaggressions Uses increasingly hostile language when blaming those who are different (e.g. 'Go back to your own country') Considers those who are different to be less than human (e.g. savages, animals) Exhibits increased undermining, harrassment and targeting of those who are different Uses gaslighting and clever arguments designed to portray their group as victims	Intolerant and racist Able to incite hatred and violence Exhibits direct verbal and physical aggression Talks of conspiracy theories Use of extreme racial slurs and inciting of racial hared Exhibits increased harrassment, bullying and victimisation	At risk of extremism and terrorism Exhibits strategic racism Exhibits audience-shaping tactics and behaviours to stop the advancement of those who are different Uses position to influence Finds ways to minimise the power and influence of ethnic minorities and dismisses any disparities that exist amongst groups Able to incite violence

with racism. Targeting boards seems to be genius. I'm interested to see if there is more room for me to grow and whether I am as far out of all the caves as I think I am.

What perpetuates and keeps us stuck within our caves of privilege?

When we live deep within a cave (or caves) of privilege, we may convince ourselves that there is strength in difference. This is something that Malorie Blackman wrote about in her novel, *Noughts and Crosses*, in 2001. We tell ourselves that it is important to construct 'systems' around our differences. Our negative automatic thoughts and 'delusions' and our fear of 'other' and 'that which is different' keep us stuck in those caves.

At stage + 1 and – 1 of the Six Stages Framework, we are oblivious and uninterested in the experiences of others, and see nothing wrong with our caves as we continue to furnish and decorate them. Our behaviours and responses to racial issues at this stage include remaining silent, keeping our heads down, and hoping that 'uncomfortable' conversations will end, or we may find ways to block them and divert to 'safer' topics.

However, if we remain at this stage for too long, we may slip deeper into the cave and proceed down the negative axis as our values and beliefs become more entrenched. When this starts to happen, we become more vulnerable to the negative influences of others and to what we are told on social media (Fig. 1).

The Six Stages Framework programme and training provides advice on how to begin deconstructing and dismantling 'caves of privilege', both our own and those of others. It increases understanding of how someone gets into a cave by considering early experiences and the role of the media and other people in shaping biases and prejudices. The conceptual framework allows individuals to determine how deeply they are within their caves. Some important questions are asked, such as:

- What things have you done (and continue to do) that keep you deep inside your cave?
- What things reinforce your perceptions, beliefs, prejudices and 'delusions'?
- What are the payoffs for you?
- Who do you spend your time with?
- What new perspectives, support or challenges do you get from other people?

This is not an accusatory process but one of self-learning, to help you understand how you have come to hold certain views and beliefs.

Using conversations on race to shift existing limiting paradigms

I recently heard Michael Beckwith, a 'New-Thought' minister and the author and founder of the Agape International Spiritual Center in Beverly Hills, California (Wikipedia)

Fig. 5: Spectrum of racism on the positive axis of the Six Stages Framework.

Racial intolerance and prejudice		Increasing awareness	Challenging and dealing with racism		Leadership action
Exhibits indirect racism Exhibits biases and prejudices Thinks in and uses stereotypes Displays microaggressions Uses racial slurs Engages in gaslighting Asks so- called 'dumb questions'	Exhibits and unaware of own and others' biases Thinks in and uses stereotypes Displays microaggressions Uses racial slurs and excuses it as just banter Makes 'innocent' jokes about differences that undermine and act as put-downs Uses casual racist put-downs veiled as humour, jokes and 'just banter'	Recognises biases and prejudice Owns up to own biases Feels helpless to act Recognises that humour is often used to disguise racial stereo-types and racism Recognises the power of language and undermining effects	Understands about biases and stereotypes Recognises prejudice and discrimination Offers some challenges Recognises racial slurs and put-downs Recognises microaggressions and gaslighting	Consistently recognises microaggressions Understands and challenges biases and prejudice Recognises and speaks up against systemic and institutional racism Recognises differential treatment and racial disparities and outcomes	Understands all forms of racial prejudice, discrimination and racism including institutional racism Is able to deal with all forms of racism including institutional racism Able to influence others Understands and recognises intersectionality and other forms of prejudice and discrimination Understands and can link values-based leadership to DEI principles, strategy and outcomes

expressing a sentiment that resonated with some of my work. He said that sometimes we aren't able to comprehend certain things because they're beyond our current paradigm, and added:

> *We need to engage in mature communication with each other, with humanity at the centre. Being able to interact and communicate openly and honestly enables us to all gain from being together on this planet.*

Some paradigms are limiting and can keep us engaged in conversations that are limiting – and therefore not fit for purpose. It is clear that the world is crying out for humanity to create new conversations and new paradigms, requiring new insights to shift existing cultural norms and behaviours. If we are brave enough to have these conversations, we will be able to script a new shared language so that we can all appreciate what racism is and what it looks like – so that, when children and young people are asked (by adults) 'Is that racism?', they will be able to answer 'yes' or 'no' and give clear reasons.

I truly believe that recent events have given us a fresh opportunity to develop a higher level of consciousness, unity and compassion, and I hope that in the years to come, the focus of the media will go through a paradigm shift – one in which people honestly interact with one another regardless of race, gender or disability, where brave conversations about differences are commonplace, where people are honest and willing to change, and organisations seek out new-age diversity coaching or therapy for their employees and their organisation as a whole. To achieve this, we must all be willing to do the work and challenge our existing paradigms and realities. Unless we do so, we risk living in an ever-more polarised world.

The Six Stages Framework helps individuals to evolve as a 'self', activating their understanding of empathy and compassion. When they do this, their character shifts. They want to be the best version of themselves, even in the face of others who don't want to see or accept others' rights exist in this world, or who don't recognise the injustice and inequity that is a daily part of the lives of others. The framework supports individuals to rise above the 'limitations' and 'labels' (Delgaudio, 2021) that others have imposed on us and to be defined by our true identities, by who we are. According to Delgaudio, it allows us:

> *... to be defined by what people see and what people don't see.*

It does this by connecting our experiences as human beings and helping us to truly see each other with compassion and empathy. The Six Stages Framework also helps to transform our relationships with people who are close to and different from us. It allows us to shift our behaviours a little bit at a time – a process that psychologists call 'behavioural modification'. These small changes allow us to interact differently with others. We get to change our thinking and mental habits, and the habitual ways we speak to and interact with others. We stretch ourselves beyond our comfort zones. It is possible for someone to be at different levels of the Six Stages Framework in different areas of functioning, but the overall aim of the programme is designed to help us get to Stage +6 of the framework in all areas. However, it is not a linear model – it is dynamic and fluid, as shown in Figs 7–8.

Using the Six Stages Framework and the prejudice–racism spectrum as assessment tools

Identifying where individuals or organisations are on the prejudice–racism spectrum and the Six Stages Framework makes room for conversations on exploring values, beliefs and behaviours and, ultimately, promotes change. This work can be done in schools, universities and the workplace through supervision, mentoring and in the corporate world through coaching. It can also be used in leadership training and evaluations.

The Six Stages Framework and the prejudice–racism spectrum, if used sensitively as learning tools, reduces defensiveness and avoids concerns about being labelled a 'racist' or not. They become tools for change, and can be used for assessment, goal-setting and self-monitoring in an open and ongoing way. The facilitate genuine conversations in which individuals are supported to explore their position on the spectrum or framework and the reasons why. Anyone can use them including those who are intolerant of differences and those who are experiencing discrimination and racism. Doing the work allows individuals to better initiate conversations, drawing from others' behaviours and experiences and considering these alongside their own beliefs, attitudes and interpretation of events; it also helps avoid the escalation of events and complaints.

This work must be carried out by those who are trained in the use of the Six Stages Framework, who are skilled in psychological assessments and formulations, such as psychologists with DEI expertise or those specifically trained in DEI and the use of the assessments, such as DEI consultants. These practitioners and consultants conduct the assessments, set goals, monitor progress and provide feedback. The assessments can be carried out at individual or organisational level. As Nina Simonds, Leadership Facilitator and Executive Coach, said in August 2021, when I shared my ideas about the framework and prejudice–racism spectrum:

> *I appreciate this framework and what it offers us – the opportunity to be curious about our internalized racism and empathetic of others. When we view racism on a spectrum rather than as a binary choice, we have more room for learning and curiosity.*

Fig. 6: The full prejudice–racism equity spectrum.

Racial intolerance and prejudice		Indirect racism	Increasing intolerance and direct racism		Leadership action
Exhibits indirect racism Exhibits biases and prejudice Thinks in and uses stereotypes Asks so-called 'dumb questions' Makes 'innocent' jokes about differences that under-mine and act as put-downs	Exhibits indirect racism Exhibits biases and prejudices Thinks in and uses stereotypes Exhibits micro-aggressions Uses racial slurs and casual racist remarks Uses gaslighting	Exhibits direct and indirect racism Exhibits increasing intolerance When called out, excuses behaviour as 'just banter' Undermines those who are different (e.g. makes disparaging comments)	Exhibits direct and indirect racism Exhibits micro-aggressions Increasingly hostile lang-uage when blaming those who are different (e.g. 'Go back to your own country') Considers those who are different to be less than human (e.g. savages, animals) Increased undermining, harrassment and targeting of those who are different Uses gaslight-ing and clever arguments designed to portray their group as victims	Intolerant and racist Able to incite hatred and violence Exhibits direct verbal and physical aggression Talks of conspiracy theories Use of extreme racial slurs and inciting of racial hared Exhibits increased harrassment, bullying and victimisation of those who are different	At risk of extremism and terrorism Exhibits strategic racism Exhibits audience-shaping tactics and behaviours to stop the advancement of those who are different Uses position to influence Finds ways to minimise the power and influence of ethnic minorities and dismisses any dispari-ties that exist among groups Able to incite violence

Racial intolerance and prejudice		Increasing awareness	Challenging and dealing with racism		Leadership action
Exhibits indirect racism Exhibits biases and prejudices Thinks in and uses stereotypes Displays micro-aggressions Uses racial slurs Engages in gaslighting Asks so-called 'dumb questions'	Exhibits and unaware of own and others' biases Thinks in and uses stereotypes Displays micro-aggressions Uses racial slurs and excuses it as 'just banter' Makes 'innocent' jokes about differences that undermine and act as put-downs Uses casual racist put-downs veiled as humour, jokes and 'just banter'	Recognises biases and prejudice Owns up to own biases Feels helpless to act Recognises that humour is often used to disguise racial stereotypes and racism Recognises the power of language and undermining effects	Understands about biases and stereotypes Recognises prejudice and discrimination Offers some challenges Recognises racial slurs and put-downs Recognises micro-aggressions and gaslighting	Consistently recognises micro-aggressions Understands and challenges biases and prejudice Recognises and speaks up against systemic and institutional racism Recognises differential treatment and racial disparities and outcomes	Understands all forms of racial prejudice, discrimination and racism, including institutional racism Is able to deal with all forms of racism, including institutional racism Is able to influence others Understands and recognises intersectionality and other forms of prejudice and discrimination Understands and can link values-based leadership to DEI principles, strategy and outcomes

Fig. 7: The dynamic and fluid nature of the negative axis of the Six Stages Framework.

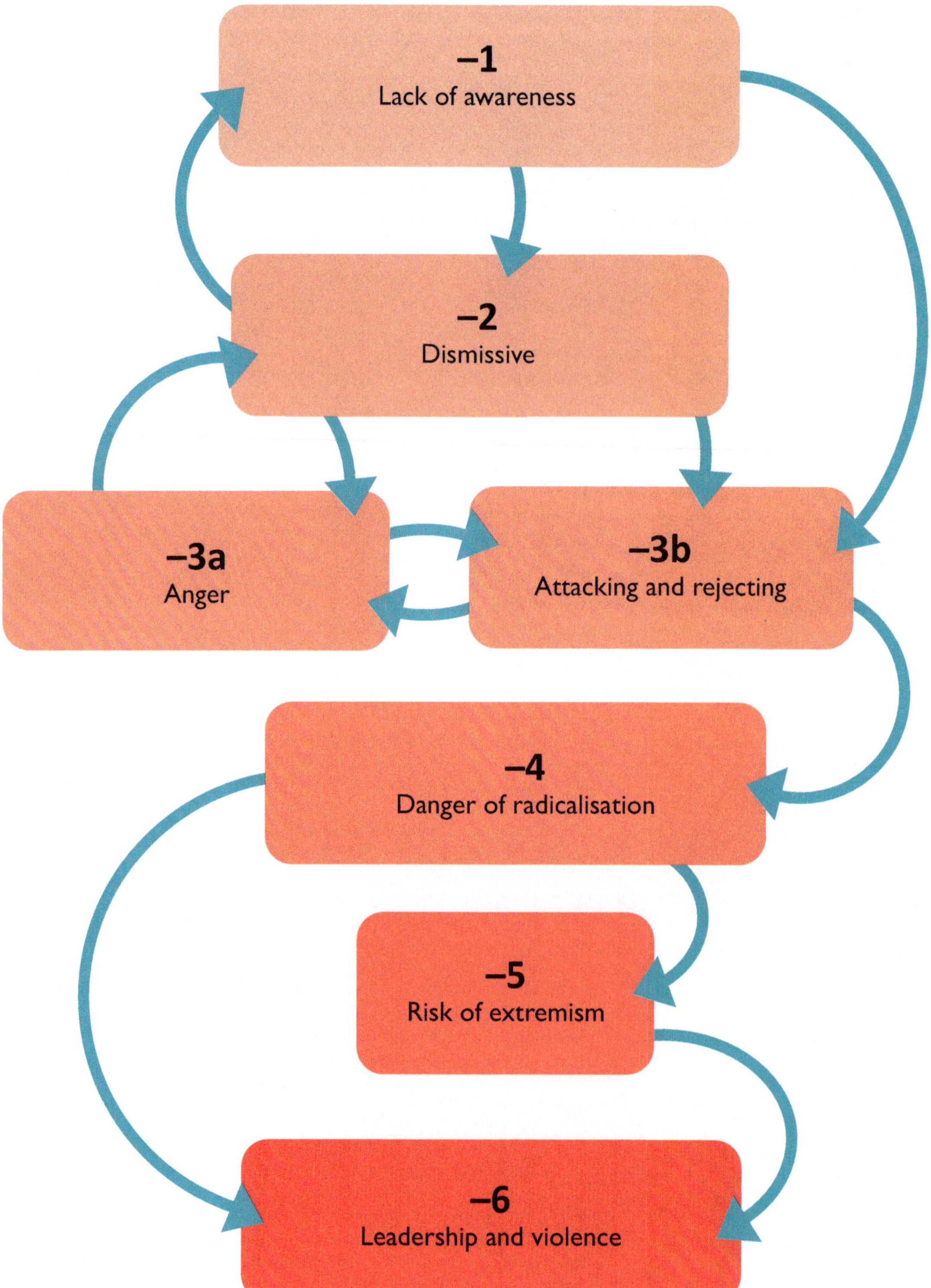

Fig. 8: The dynamic and fluid nature of the positive axis of the Six Stages Framework.

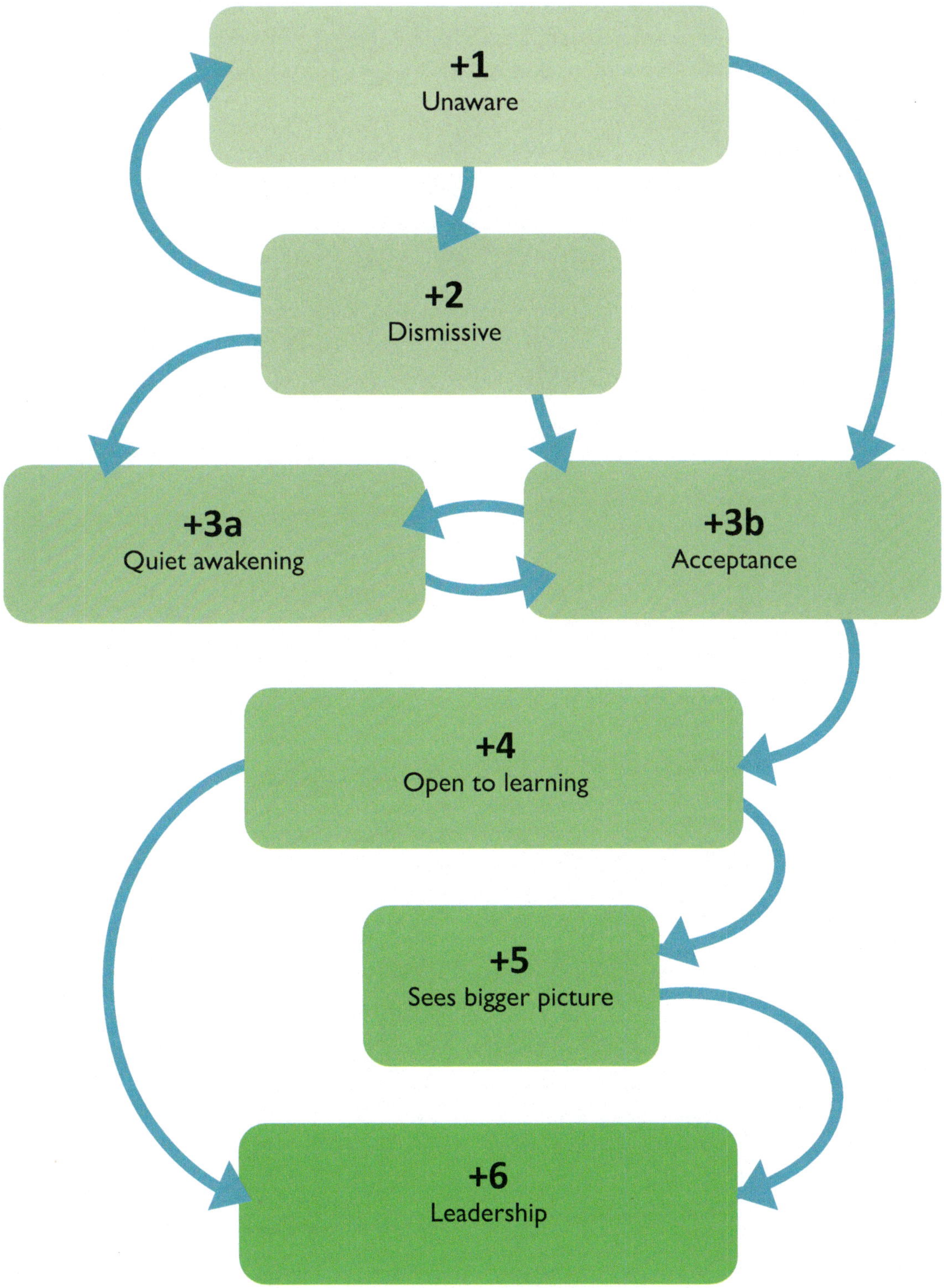

The Six Stages Framework is a call to action

Everyone has a role to play in encouraging conversations to combat prejudice, discrimination and racism; whether this is parents in the home, friends socialising in the community, teachers within schools, lecturers within colleges/ universities, managers and leaders in the workplace, chairs of cricket boards, those within football grounds or those within the police force or within governments.

The Six Stages Framework is an action-based positive tool that will speak to many people and provide the language many people feel that they don't have to speak about their own biases and racism. "What is special about the Six Stages Framework, is that it is a positive, action-based, non-judgemental tool that is essential to addressing sensitive topics.

Aishling Dempsey, MSc Clinical Health Psychology student/ Honorary Psychology Assistant, Inclusion Psychologists Ltd.

DEI issues—organisational factors

8

A commitment to diversity and inclusion is not enough

Following George Floyd's murder, many organisations were quick to express their commitment to racial equity, diversity and inclusion. Reading their posts and threads on professional forums, as well as individual statements by businesses, I thought *here we go again*.

Unfortunately, anti-racism statements are like the old equal opportunities policies that languished for years in dusty filing cabinets, long forgotten. It is common for people to say all the right things, but rarely do their words match their actions.

The truth is that commitments like these to equality and diversity and position statements are not enough – because nothing seems to change! What is required are tangible and practical actions that challenge the fabric of institutional and organisational racism. The Charity Commission (2017) pointed the spotlight on the slow rate of change in board-level diversity, and others have raised similar concerns regarding public and corporate boards (Harley-McKeown, 2021; Hopke, 2021). This is why the Six Stages Framework was originally developed. Rather than just 'making a commitment', there is an urgent need to truly understand the lived experiences of black and minority ethnic people, professionals and senior managers, and to interrogate existing and new data.

In 'First letter to white educational psychologists: We can't breathe – Black Lives Matter' (M'gadzah, 2020), I explained that, as a profession, psychologists should seize the opportunities that arose after George Floyd's killing or else continue to languish in their ivory towers, telling themselves that racism exists everywhere other than their own profession.

It is regrettable and somewhat surprising that this is not the case. It has been said that the Royal family should do the same, seeing the interview by Harry and Meghan as an opportunity to progress towards true racial equity, diversity and inclusion.

I was heartened to hear that the Royal family are taking steps to review DEI issues, perhaps appointing a diversity chief to acknowledge that more must be done, with a review designed to assess and improve representation across the Royal household (Giordano, 2021). This may be a positive step, but only time will tell whether it is a sign of real change or a way of being seen to be 'doing something'.

According to Baroness Valerie Amos at the School of Oriental Studies (SOAS, 2020), deep inequalities exist within society and these are exacerbated by racism. I believe this is true, and last year I wrote this in one of my letters (M'gadzah, 2020) to the Educational Psychologists Forum (including a message of hope):

> *We can pretend as a society that these problems of racial injustice do not exist in the UK, only in America, and spend time on Working parties and Reviews and hope that by the time they are finished, things will have moved on and the cries for change will have stopped – some may say: We will have weathered the storm! Things can go back to normal until next time. However, we will be ready with more excuses and even more skilled at strategies such as ignoring the discussions and hiding in the shadows of silence next time round. ... Perhaps the protests we have seen about racial justice are really a new beginning, and perhaps the current global momentum will propel different professional groups and businesses into action – with tangible results – and this time things will be different. Perhaps soon we will all be able to breathe and, even more importantly, young black and minority ethnic employees, such as educational psychologists joining the psychology profession, will not suffer the experiences that many of us have.*

Lucy Harley-McKeown, in her article dated June 2021, reported that:

> *Racial discrimination is still rife in UK businesses, despite targeted support for ethnic minorities. Despite this progress, however, Henley's research showed there are still fundamental issues to address in eliminating racism in the workplace.*

She described a new report called *The Equity Effect* produced by Henley Business School, which found that black employees are the 'worst off', stating that Henley's research showed:

> *... there are still fundamental issues to address in eliminating racism in the workplace.*

She further commented:

> *Black employees are more than twice as likely to experience racial discrimination compared to Asians and mixed ethnic minorities (19% vs 9% and 8%). In terms of how this manifests, the leading form of discriminatory action cited by ethnic minorities is discrimination in work allocation (41%). Verbal abuse is second (33%), and following this, is inappropriate and unfair application of work policies or rules (29%). When it comes to recognising the racial inequity, White business leaders are significantly less likely to have seen discrimination in their organisation in comparison to those from an ethnic minority background (30% vs 47%). It therefore doesn't bode well that 70% of those surveyed said their senior leadership was White.*

The report found that businesses that actively confront inequity and racism and that use practical measures:

> *... can expect to see an improvement in their employees' job satisfaction, loyalty, creativity and, ultimately, value, recording an average revenue 58% higher than those who did not.*

Describing a conversation with a leading researcher, Dr Naeema Pasha, Director of EDI at Henley Business School, Fitzgerald said this:

> *Racial equity and business success should not be separate conversations. It is critical to any organisation wanting to achieve its aims and ambitions in this challenging world of work. ... Of course, we all want to say that racism has no place in business, education or society. But the experience of the pandemic and social movements like Black Lives Matter have shown us that we need to shift our organisational, cultural thinking to ensure we work on racial equity – not just because it is a good thing or seen as worthy, but because it is valuable and essential to organisational success.*

Public stands against racism—posturing and position statements will not achieve the change required

At the start of 2021, I was asked by a colleague about the statements that were put out by multiple organisations following the killing of George Floyd and the subsequent protests. The question was, *what would you consider intentional versus performative, unintentional damage control?*

I replied that I was not surprised by companies wanting to be seen as taking a public stand against racial injustice and racism. For some, it seemed to be a case of immediate damage control, as evidenced by statements such as "racism has no place in our society" from the Association of Educational Psychologists (AEP), leading some of us to ask, "What about within our profession?" (M'gadzah, 2020). I explained how many organisations, up until that point, including the AEP, had refused or failed to address racial inequality but were then quick to be *seen* to be making the right moves.

However, others – like Nike and Ben & Jerry's – quickly took action, offering financial support to fight racial injustice. Survey Monkey went even further, stating on the CNN News in 2020:

> *If an organization we do business with isn't making the values we believe are a priority, we will do business elsewhere.*

It is encouraging that McDonald's chain of fast-food restaurants reported linking its executive-officer bonuses to diversity goals and targets. Starbucks seems to be doing something similar, but the details are not yet available (Russ, 2021).

This is what I mean by taking meaningful action – not just making statements or setting up working parties or commissions, which have questionable findings and provide no clear new direction or solutions. There is still a lot of posturing (and pretence) about eliciting change, but in the absence of empathy or trust.

Organisations like to put out position statements while their own practices are accused of perpetuating discrimination, racism and intolerance. We must all be open and transparent and start talking about organisations like this (including senior leaders and unions that fail to investigate false allegations against black managers), even if means naming and shaming them. And we must celebrate those who do the right things. We need to put a stop to empty posturing, to just saying the right things, and encourage pledges to challenge structural racism, such as one recently posted by the AEP.

Unfortunately, during more than thirty years in the psychology profession, I have seen many working parties and pledges come and go, so I only believe the sincerity of such efforts based on results and progress within the profession and other organisations, including the UK Government and Royal family.

Instead we must start *doing* – and *thinking* about what we are doing and reviewing what we have already done. All organisations need to recognise and accept that the work involved in racial equity and inclusion begins with honesty – first and foremost – and an acknowledgement of the complexities of racism. They need to put their hands up and admit when they've got it wrong. All of us (as individuals and as organisations) should admit our thoughts, biases and prejudices and call out the cultures that exist and serve to perpetuate racism and negative outcomes for black and minority ethnic groups. We need to challenge ourselves, and others, to deal with these issues. We need to speak up within our organisations and support others to do the same. I saw Ken Chenault, former CEO of American Express, speaking on CNN in April 2021. He said that since George Floyd's death, cooperate America has 'stepped up'; he spoke of the joint responsibility of corporations and stakeholders in achieving change:

> *I think it's not just the awareness, it's the understanding that corporations exist because society allows us to exist and we need to do what it takes to improve society and the recognition that race is America's greatest unsolved problem. We need all stakeholders in our society to be focused on bringing about true racial equality and economic opportunity for all and justice for all.*

What are the reasons for diversifying companies—furthering racial justice by doing the right thing or is it for profit lines?

Sarah Todd (2021) explored the financial benefits of diversity, citing three McKinsey studies that indicate links between diversity in the workplace and higher company profits.

> *Key to the popularization of this idea are three McKinsey studies released in 2015, 2018, and 2020, which showed that companies with greater racial, ethnic, and gender diversity in their leadership tended to perform better financially.*

She mentioned recent academic research by Hand and Green (2021), commenting:

> *... academic research is less clear on whether there is any relationship between diverse leadership and company profits—let alone a causal one. The researchers did not find a link between racial and ethnic diversity and financial performance.*

As she explained, the McKinsey studies did not establish causation but rather a correlation in the role that inclusive and fair environments play in a company's success:

> *Scholarly researchers have rarely found that increased diversity leads to improved financial outcomes', Ely and Thomas explain in a 2020 article for the Harvard Business Review. 'They have found that it leads to higher-quality work, better decision-making, greater team satisfaction, and more equality—under certain circumstances. Although those outcomes could conceivably make some aspects of the business more profitable, they would need to be extraordinarily consequential to affect a firm's bottom line.*

She also observed that:

> *McKinsey's studies aren't suggesting that profits are the only reason to invest in diversity. A 2020 opinion piece by the firm, tied to its most recent diversity report, highlighted the ways in which companies that prioritise diversity are likely to benefit from better decision-making, more innovation, and higher employee satisfaction.*

Her article suggested that while profit lines are important for organisations, the focus of encouraging greater diversity is intrinsic motivation.

> *Diversifying companies as a means of furthering racial justice and gender equality is an extremely meaningful cause, she commented, that is, simply calling companies to do so because it's the right thing to do.*

Are organisations ready for real change?

It is my opinion that more organisations are ready to make real changes, but some continue with their posturing, giving the impression that they are doing the right things in order to preserve their image. They see work in this area as a 'box-ticking' exercise. Others are being forced to make changes by their stakeholders and partners. It seems that there is real potential for change in many organisations, and the energy and emotion generated to date has started 'diversity wheels' turning worldwide.

There is yet more energy coming from young people, who are far less tolerant of social and racial injustice. I think the letter 'e' in the word *energy* indicates *emotion*, and the 'e' in *emotion* signifies *empathy*. In DEI work, it is vital to be aware of emotional intelligence (M'gadzah, 2011) and to know that the conversations we have with our teams enhance (or reduce) the energy within an organisation. Thus we need to support all organisations (particularly those that are sitting on the fence) to 'build bridges of empathy' (M'gadzah, 2021) when working with their employees, and to promote belonging, mental health and good outcomes (City Mental Health Alliance, 2021). There are a number of factors to consider with respect to emotional intelligence when working with organisations. These include:

- supporting people to cut their attachments and to emerge from their caves
- engaging and asking questions (in no-blame and safe environments)
- perceiving, using, understanding and managing emotions

- fostering self-awareness and understanding of one's own emotions
- self-managing and regulating one's own emotions and behaviours
- understanding emotions of others and perceiving and interpreting emotional cues
- developing social emotional skills and empathy
- understanding how our emotions impact our thinking and our behaviour.

Successful organisations should have clear lines of accountability, whereby senior leaders oversee and assume responsibility for doing the work in this area. Some organisations consider that focusing on unconscious-bias training will address this issues, however I have seen black and minority ethnic staff appointed as DEI leads who received very little support or training, with no strategy, and who feel overwhelmed.

Other organisations continue to have DEI resource groups but do not involve senior leaders, which results in little or no real change. Someone contacted me recently about coaching and said to me:

> *We have done some anti-racism training – but now what? Nothing seems to have changed.*

This is typical among organisations that are overwhelmed by the many challenges they face, and where training is viewed as a check-box exercise. Some report that their staff became upset by in-house training, and are left feeling worse afterwards. The truth is that, if not delivered carefully, this kind of training can cause more harm than good.

Organisations that tackle DEI issues well should be acknowledged for their efforts, but they also need support in recognising that the work is complex and can be very emotionally charged. The process of sharing and reflecting on personal and professional journeys requires careful guidance and facilitation.

My advice for organisations, therefore, is to seek out suitably skilled expertise, to help their teams reflect on and manage some of the issues and tensions that inevitably arise; they should always be made aware of the risks and be mindful – in particular – of the mental health needs of their staff (especially those who are from black and minority ethnic groups). They need to appreciate the emotional toll this work can have when individuals are asked to open painful wounds.

What else is needed to support organisations with racial equity and inclusion?

Now, more than ever, is the time to provide initiatives that encourage businesses and organisations to network about DEI (see the *Race Equality Matters* website). Networking allows them to share their work, which is crucial for galvanising other organisations that do not yet recognise the issues. Other factors to consider when working in DEI are:

- greater scientific rigour
- best-practice guidelines
- agreed standards for DEI consultants

- evidence-based tools (e.g. established DEI frameworks)
- research on understanding and assessing attitudes, behaviours and responses to racism using tools such as the Six Stages Framework.

Businesses have to consider policies designed to strengthen the economy and their businesses; it is clear that diversity and inclusion policies that ensure a place for everyone strengthen businesses. But awareness-raising and reflection are only the first steps in dealing with racial injustice and inequality; what must follow are steps to take action and set tangible goals. They include measuring the energy and motion of a company's 'diversity wheels', given that some wheels are firmly stuck, and others are only slowly churning into action. Where there is a real commitment to change, the wheels turn freely and propel the organisation forwards at some pace!

What does it take and what are the costs if we fail to do this work and achieve change?

In January 2021, I posted a blog asking, "So what does it take and what are the costs if we fail to do this work?". With all the conversations and protests that took place following George Floyd's death, and the attacks on the US Capitol, some said it was a time for 'healing'. However, before healing can begin, there is work to do that includes 'building bridges of empathy' (M'gadzah, 2020), putting ourselves in someone else's shoes (like those of the police officers who battled with protesters at the Capitol, like Brian Sicknick who later died) to imagine how they must have felt when desperately trying to hold back the mob.

We need to be able to talk honestly about trust, and about building trust with each other, across different racial groups and at work. And we need to be sure our colleagues will support us – that they will 'have our back'. These are common concerns among those who are in the minority, or who experience racism in the workplace. It is only when we practise building 'bridges of empathy' and promote an understanding of what it's like for someone who is different that the real healing can begin.

Each one of us must be able to reflect their own biases, prejudices and negative automatic thoughts about others who are different. We all have them, these thoughts, so it is important to recognise them before considering their impact, and before they become deep-seated prejudices or racism.

Speaking on the CNN *Amanpour* news in March 2021, economist Heather McGhee explained how racism exacerbates inequalities, not just for 'people of colour' but for white people as well. She outlined what she sees as the 'costs' if we do not do this work – how racism affects us all – and how we can prosper together. She asserted:

> *What is driving inequalities is racism and American dysfunction is as a result of racism in our politics and in our policy-making.*

She also shared the story of 'brave' Gary, who she talked to during a television programme on the C-Span Public Affairs Network. Gary said:

> *I was hoping you guys would help me change my mind about some things. I'm a white male and I'm prejudiced. What can I do to change and to be a better American?*

He went on to share intricate details of his prejudices, including his views on black men, drugs and crime. McGhee was quite taken aback, but then shocked viewers by thank thanking him:

> *Thank you so much for being honest and for opening up this conversation because it's simply one of the most important ones we have to have in this country. So your ability to say that 'this is what I have, I have these fears and prejudices and I want to get over them' is one of the most powerful things we can do right now at this moment in our history.*

She thanked him for admitting his prejudices and for wanting to change – clearly impressed by his belief that overcoming prejudice would make him a better American. She later said on CNN in 2021,

> *Since then he has been on this journey of unlearning a lot of the received stereotypes that are marketed so aggressively to white men, e.g. that the progress of people of colour is coming at the white man's expense.*

They have since become friends, as Gary continues on his journey to change. Of this, she said,

> *It's helped me see that there is the possibility of human transformation. ... Racism does not have to be about conflict. People were expecting a conflict because when you see race on cable TV news you see conflict.*

As I listened to her talking, I thought we should all be more like Gary and McGhee, asking basic questions about how we can change and improve ourselves so we can relate more effectively to those who are different; and we should also strive to take the conflict out of discussions on race, approaching them instead non-judgementally and empathetically.

Racism costs everyone—not just black and ethnic minority people

Heather McGhee also gave a Ted Talk in 2020, in which she referred to Gary:

> *I think people were surprised that a black woman would show such compassion for prejudiced white men and they were surprised that the white man would admit his bias on live television. ... He said it had been like someone had wiped the window and let the light in. ... His prejudice had caused him to suffer fear, anxiety and isolation. Racism is bad for white people too – it backfires on the privileged.*

She described this in the context of the financial crisis in America, how racism can "backfire on the entire country".

Some people believe that if you uplift black people, you're downing white people, black anathema narrators are considered to be a drain on the town.

She also referred to the response to segregation orders in Montgomery Alabama back in 1959, which attempted to stop black people from swimming in the town's public pool. Municipalities drained the pools and closed parks and other public amenities because they did not want to share them with black people. McGhee outlined the costs of society being divided:

It costs so much to remain divided. This is zero-sum thinking that what's good for one group just comes at the expense of another group. It's time to reject that old paradigm and realise that our fates are linked. An injury to one is an injury to all. We can keep pretending that we are not all on the same team; we can keep sabotaging our success and hamstringing out on players. Or we can let the proximity of so much difference reveal our common humanity and we can finally invest in our greatest asset, our people, all of our people.

Viewing diversity as a superpower—setting aside prejudice and stereotypes for the greater good

Our diversity could be a superpower but racism has been used as a divide and conquer weapon that impoverishes as all—McGhee 2021

McGhee has talked about the possibility of a public transformation, and how we have to work together to address racism in order to address the issues that are holding America back. Her observations make it clear that segregation comes with a cost to us all, and damages people and whole economies. On the subject of the zero-sum paradigm, she said:

It's where people think that equality means that someone else is going to benefit at my expense.

She also referred to the 'solidarity dividend' – which occurs when people come together across lines of race and reject zero-sum politics:

Can we manage to put aside stereotypes and recognise that we all deserve the kinds of investments that we know create broad economic security. And yes, we can – in fact we cannot afford not to. What unites us is so much more than what divides us.

We see similar discussions about the need for a global solidarity dividend in relation, for example, to the sharing of Covid-19 vaccines, recognising that no single country is safe from the virus until the whole world is safe.

It is critical to have these conversations within the workplace, to fully explore people's fears. The Six Stages Framework provides a structure for doing this, and by using the Six Stages diversity assessments and developmental matrices, managers will be supported to have these conversations with their staff, thus moving them through the next stages of their journey to understand and deal more effectively with racial differences, divides and racism.

On compassion, empathy and humanity—black people are human beings (not animals)

Many of us watched the trial of Derek Chauvin, the US police officer found guilty of killing George Floyd – tough viewing for black, white and other ethnic minority groups. In Belgium, the deaths of young black men at the hands of the police also led to accusations against the police for acting with impunity; anti-police protests followed and hundreds were detained. The Belgian police unions say there may be individuals who are racist amongst their ranks, but that accusations of institutional racism are unfair; they deny they are a racist force.

Does any of this sound familiar? How many organisations out there admit to the existence of institutional racism within their walls? My experience is that the standard response of police departments, the Society of British Editors, educational institutions, the Royal family, and the UK Government seems to be to deny any racist intent.

In Belgium, a human rights lawyer called Alexis Deswaef talked about one of the young men in Belguim (Ibrahima B) who died at the hands of the police in January 2021. In April 2021, he stated:

> *All the police officers are white and he was black and they're saying he's crying like an animal. If the person had been white they would never have said that. They would've understood that he was crying because he was dying and he was suffocating.*

Ibrahima B's sister said of her brother:

> *... they may not have been able to save him but they could have helped him. They wouldn't have left him lying on the floor for seven minutes without help if he was white.*

Are there parallels, here, with the killing of George Floyd? Where is the humanity in these officers? What happens in these moments, and how can they be so unmoved by the suffering of another human being? On CNN, Ana Navarro, a political commentator, remarked:

> *... this is not just black people's problem. This is an issue about humanity and it affects us all – not just black people. ... If this had been a person standing on the neck of an animal or kneeling on the neck of an animal, white people and American people would be outraged. Yet because this is a black person, it is seen as it is nothing to do with us and we can look the other way.*

Her message was clear – white people cannot afford to look the other way because these are issues about humanity and not just issues for black people. She continued:

> *... white people need to watch the Derek Chauvin trial and see what happened so that they can understand why black people feel the way they do and so that they can understand the history of the hurt and pain and emotional baggage that some say black people carry.*

Protecting black and ethnic minority peoples' mental health

BraVada Garrett Akinsanya is the founder of the African–American Child Wellness Institute She was interviewed on CNN news in April 2021, where she was asked about black people who avoid watching the news because they cannot bear to witness yet more black people being in pain or being killed. She spoke about their need to protect their mental health at the same time as engaging with these constant messages of suffering. This isn't an easy balance to achieve. The same can be said of Asian people in the face of rising Asian hate crimes. BraVada advised black people to:

> *... take small doses of the news and not overexpose [themselves] to it.*

The avoidance of such coverage is in itself indicative of post-traumatic stress disorder (PTSD), so it is important to look out for the signs and symptoms in those who may be affected, so they can be signposted to appropriate support, such as the Association of Black Psychologists. Now – more than ever – it is essential that black, white, Asian and people of other ethnicities:

- talk about their feelings about the racism they experience and witness
- talk about the emotions that the images stir up
- do not suffer in silence or tell themselves they are unaffected by what is going on around them
- talk about what is happening in their communities and around the world
- stand up and challenge bias and discrimination wherever they see it
- do not remain silent.

When the UN Secretary General, António Guterres, was asked what lessons he hopes the world has learnt from the Covid pandemic, he responded:

> *The biggest lesson is to understand how fragile we are as a global society; fragile in relation to the pandemic; fragile in relation to the global space, climate change and global security. ... When we are humble enough to recognize how fragile we are, I hope we will recognise that we need global solidarity to face the challenges that are so clear in this world.*

I would assert that a key global challenge is the hate, bias and discrimination we continue to witness towards black and minority ethnic groups and those who are different. This includes the rise in Asian and antisemitic hate crimes. Such work must begin in our communities and workplaces, and we need to be 'brave' enough to see and accept that racism exists and to call it out when we see it. It is our duty to humanity, whatever our colour or cultural background. We have to be alert to people's belief systems and behaviours, and notice when they are taking a negative trajectory along the Six Stages negative axis – where beliefs and behaviours become more entrenched and put our communities at risk. We cannot turn the other way; there are real negative consequences when we allow seeds of hate to flourish, regardless of a person's colour or ethnic background, or their position or status. We have seen examples of negative behaviours among politicians in the USA and worldwide.

I can't help thinking how disingenuous it is of the UK Government in their Commission Report (2021), and other organisations, to deny the existence of racism – institutional or otherwise. We all have a responsibility in eradicating it. We all need to wake up and face the reality of the challenges that lie ahead, both within our communities and globally – that is the reality of racism. It doesn't just affect black or Asian people; it affects us all. As I keep saying:

Without empathy and compassion we are nothing but animals.

The death of George Floyd and reactions to Chauvin's sentence

On 25 June 2021, Derek Chauvin was sentenced to twenty-two and a half years imprisonment and is likely to serve fifteen years of that, depending on good behaviour. The judge said that Chauvin treated George Floyd without respect, and that he denied him the dignity owed to all human beings. It is clear from recent events, and in particular the killing of George Floyd, that black people in both the USA and UK are reacting to historical trauma and the impact of years of police brutality and social injustice. Many have said Chauvin's sentence was too lenient, given the cruel nature of his crime and the fact that it was committed in front of children and other police officers. They also consider it to be out of line with what a black person would receive for a similar crime.

The judge who passed the sentence recognised how difficult George Floyd's killing and the trial had been for the Floyd family but explained that he was not going to be influenced by emotions or sympathy but rather the letter of the law. Keith Ellison, Minnesota Attorney General, said that after the judgement many people, including police officers, called for real reform and meaningful change, for greater accountability and a law that treats everyone with dignity and respect – a law that everyone can trust. He added:

Where there's no trust, no one is safe.

According to CNN News, many are now calling for a George Floyd Act to be passed, to look at police reform across the USA. Some believe justice was not served – a man lost his life – and called the judge's sentencing disrespectful to George Floyd's family and the black community as a whole. Others say it is a beginning, because it actually led to the sentencing of a police officer. But the civil rights leader Reverend Al Sharpton had this to say:

... one sentence does not solve a nation's criminal justice problem.

A psychologist called Alfiee Breland-Noble explained that we will never know the full extent of the family's pain or trauma (especially Floyd's seven-year-old daughter), but the sentence does demonstrate a sense of accountability – a small thing, but establishing accountability is part of the healing process, and it is something the family will be able to hold onto, and will allow both the family and the black community to start healing. It is a step in the right direction; in fact, it may be a turning point, according to those who acknowledged the case as a racial 'reckoning'.

Sceptics, on the other hand, believe it has had little impact on the sort of systemic change required to tackle police violence and injustice. The National Association for the Advancement of Colored People (NAACP) is the largest and oldest civil rights organisation. Its mission is to ensure the political, educational, social and economic equality of rights of all people and to eliminate race-based discrimination.

Speaking on CNN News in June 2021, Anika Bowie (Vice President of the Minneapolis NAACP) said:

> *What is needed is systemic change – real concrete change through policy, through practices, through legitimate legislation and law change, to ensure that all police officers face real consequences.*

Euro football finals—mindless racist abuse stuns the nation

On 11 July 2021, England lost the final match of the UEFA Euro football finals. The nation's hopes were pinned on the first win in 55 years. The game went to a penalty shoot off, and three black players – Bukayo Saka, Jadon Sancho and Marcus Rashford – missed their shots. The loss was upsetting loss for footballers and fans alike, and but the three men were then subjected to a tirade of online racist abuse. They were easy targets for those who wanted someone to blame. The abuse came from thousands of fans and has shone a light on the existence of racism, and highlighted the need to push organisations and the media to challenge racism at all levels. Priti Patel, the UK Home Secretary, condemned the racist abuse in a Tweet:

> *I am disgusted that England players who have given so much for our country this summer have been subject to vile racist abuse on social media. It has no place in our country and I back the police to hold those responsible accountable.*

Many people, including Tyrone Mings, an English professional footballer, then criticised Priti Patel for pretending to be disgusted by the situation, because she had failed to condemn people who booed at footballers for taking the knee. So he tweeted:

> *You don't get to stoke the fire at the beginning of the tournament by labelling our anti-racism message as 'Gesture Politics' & then pretend to be disgusted when the very thing we're campaigning against, happens.*

I responded to the media coverage of the abuse on LinkedIn (12 July 2021):

> *And some people ask, 'Why do we go on about racism – racism is a thing of the past?'. Is it? The racist abuse directed towards the three black England players following losing the European finals football match shows that racism is alive and well; it is just*

> *hidden when people choose to hide it. The trio's social media pages were flooded with racist comments, said the BBC reporting this morning. The football Association and the Prime Minister condemned the racism on social media. As I watched the penalty shoot-out I feared this would be the reaction from some England fans. The message is clear: you don't belong; you only belong when you're helping us win; but if you do not, then you're not one of us. I ask you, what messages are we sending to children in England (and around the world), and in particular to black and ethnic minority children? What messages are we sending to these football players? This team has brought the nation together. It's so diverse, with players from different backgrounds. They have taken so much action over the year to fight against racism. The Metropolitan police are reported to have said they are aware of the abuse but it is not clear at this stage if any action will be taken. Danny Mills, former England defender, speaking on BBC News this morning, asked: 'How can you go from loving the players one minute to then hating them and giving out racist abuse?' He added, 'These were not just a few fans. This was several thousand of them, dishing out racist abuse at black players. It's not enough to say that the people who sent these messages should be ashamed of themselves. More needs to be done'.*

These fans were incredibly shallow and racist – and they're the type of people I talk about in this book. Their behaviours expose their values and attitudes towards black people, and their racism is often hidden from view when they want something from black players and black people.

Unfortunately, such views are not only found among football fans – they are everywhere in society. We need to stamp them out racism and embrace conversations that explore our biases and discriminations, as well as challenge racism wherever or whenever we see it. We cannot wait until biases and prejudice become discrimination and racism. Prevention and early intervention are key, and this is where we all have a part to play, whatever colour we are. We all have to #reevaluateourbiases and take corrective action.

On 13 July 2021, Nicholas Cheffings, former Global Chair of the international law firm Hogan Lovells (who now focuses on advocacy for diversity, inclusion, anti-racism, equity and equality in business and society), posted on LinkedIn a condemnation of the racist abuse. He made it clear that this is not the world any of us want.

> *The same vile racist abuse. The same question. The same answer. Many are speaking out today in support of three fine young black men and brilliant footballers who had the misfortune to miss a penalty last night. It could have been Harry Kane or Harry Maguire but it wasn't. England lost and the racist abuse was totally predictable. The question? Do I need to add my words to those of others? The answer? Yes. Without hesitation. Old white men have to stand shoulder to shoulder with young black men to let them, and anybody else who cares to listen, know that this is not the world we want for them or for ourselves. This is not about football. It is about our society. We have to be loudly #antiracist. And to those who say #whiteprivilege is not a thing, think on this: Harry Kane and Harry Maguire didn't take that long walk to take their*

> *penalties knowing that they would face racist abuse if they missed. Perhaps Marcus Rashford, Jadon Sancho and Bukayo Saka didn't either, but perhaps they did, and who could blame them? And if they did, the racists who apparently love their country and football team made it much more likely that those penalties would be missed. Those young men need our support right now and racists need our condemnation.*

I was moved by this and posted a response:

> *Thank you so much Nicholas Cheffings for posting this and speaking up. We had a discussion just the other day on #EverydayCHPsychology and #sixstagesframework on whether people (in particular, white people) should speak out or not. Or whether this would simply add to the noise, or be seen as performative. We all agreed on the need to speak up on these issues and your post shows why and how powerful this is.*

A few days after the Euros final, a mural of Marcus Rashford in Manchester, painted in honour of his charity work, was defaced. The graffiti was quickly covered over by messages of support for the footballer. Brian Satchell talked on BBC News on 14 July about the community response, whereby hundreds of people held a virtual taking of the knee – a powerful collective response to mindless racist hate. Captain of the English team, Harry Kane, also appeared on the BBC News, stating that there's no place for those who abuse footballers. Nedum Onuoha, former professional English footballer, said it was almost like a 'reckoning'. He asked the nation: *Does this represent who you are – do you think this is okay?* On the BBC News, he said:

> *Those turning up to show support for black footballers are clearly saying 'No, it doesn't'. Many others have asked what sort of messages are we sending out to society about stamping out racism. There seems to be a shared viewed by many that in standing up against racism, the responsibility is everyone's. This is a responsibility at an individual as well as an organisational level.*

Onuoha described how people use social media to amplify racial abuse; thus we must put more responsibility on the various media outlets to make sure their products are used to amplify racist behaviours. Children, after all, are not born racist. On 12 July 2021, I was quoted in two news stories, one by Moss (2021) and one by Williams (2021), about dealing with disappointments following the Euros.

> *Dr Shungu Hilda M'gadzah, who is Director and Lead Consultant at Inclusion Psychologists Ltd, says: 'Thinking about others – in this case, the players – can help quell your own disappointment. Let's focus our attention on them and helping them recover and this will also help us recover and move on until next time'. She says: 'We will regroup and have another opportunity to bring it home. It's good to talk about feelings of disappointment and loss, especially if you shared the lead up to the game and the match itself with children, who may be less equipped to process raw emotions. It's also important that people find a way of lifting their spirits and not dwell on what could've been,' she says. 'We need to focus on what we achieved in getting so far'.*

On the same day I advertised the Everyday Psychology and Six Stages Framework clubhouse conversations , thus:

> *Understanding and dealing with racism. Let's talk about biases and prejudice. Come and share what your biases are and what biases/discrimination you have experienced.*

In the afternoon, I and attendees at the Six Stages Framework Club: Dealing with Racism reflected on the events following the infamous football match. Garry Turner, a strategic advisor who works at the intersection of design, disruption, education and innovation, joined the room and asked whether he should speak up against the recent events – whether it adds anything. His fear was that his actions would be seen as performative – just more noise. Together, we discussed his concerns and agreed that people (particularly white people) need to speak up. As long as they are authentic in their comments, they will be welcomed and well-received.

Three days later, at another Clubhouse discussion, we posed the question: "How do we deal with disappointments?". This gave us the opportunity to reflect on the difficulties some people face in dealing with disappointment and setbacks, and how someone's inability to recognise, manage and regulate their feelings and emotions, can lead to 'externalisation' of behaviours, such as lashing out at others and wanting to blame them. Other people internalise their behaviours, leading to anxiety and depression. We talked about how we start to learn to deal with disappointment from an early age, as influenced by our parents and carers and others around us.

Jim Taylor wrote an article called 'Parenting. Disappointment is good. Could disappointment in children really be healthy for them?' in 2011. He wrote:

> *You can teach your children to see stumbling blocks as opportunities to improve and grow. Offering your children a different perspective on their disappointment – I know it feels bad right now, but what can you learn from it? – gives them tools they can use to avoid or minimize their disappointment in the future, and to turn obstacles to their advantage by increasing resilience, motivation and confidence.*

I agree. Supporting children to talk about their feelings and emotions is hugely important and highlights the need for more work in schools to support children to self-regulate, and to promote emotional regulation and emotional well-being strategies (Government Green Paper, 2017). The role of emotional intelligence cannot be underestimated in this, as discussed in Chapter 4. Self-awareness, self-regulation, motivation, empathy and social skills are the cornerstones of emotional intelligence (Goleman, 2004), and are vitally important in our ability to deal with disappointment, and to understand, recognise and deal with racism. The starting point is self-awareness –being able to recognise particular feelings and being able to talk about them, instead of bottling them up.

Human resources (HR) processes

9

Selection and recruitment

In one of my blogs (M'gadzah, 2021), I referred to Doug Pagitt, Executive Director of Vote Common Good, who speaks about politics, religion, identity and kindness. He once said:

> *We choose our politicians based on their identities and then adjust our interpretations of their policies to fit. ... People think that we vote for our politicians based on policy, but it's really not the case. Whilst a lot of us want to believe that we vote for politicians because of their policies, it's really much more about identity, that we feel connected to a candidate. Very often the mistake people make is that people think that policy goes first, but that's not the case. We vote for politicians because of their identity and then we adjust our policies and our political beliefs to fit that identity.*

In my blog, I asked the question: *If we choose politicians on the basis of their identities, do we make our recruitment decisions in the same way?*. I was reminded of the time I spent on interview panels for local authorities, where I found it difficult to understand why some of my colleagues often rated black candidates as 'not appointable' when I rated them as 'good'. For example, some of them gave one particular candidate a score of 1/5, while others, including myself, scored them 4/5. This led me to suggest that we should try to understand each other's scores. One colleague told me that the candidate appeared aggressive because he constantly tapped his foot. She labelled this behaviour as aggression, whereas I labelled it as nervousness.

My experience of interview panels is that (as we are often told) some interviewers decide within seconds of a candidate walking through the door whether or not they want to appoint them. Then they spend the rest of the interview gathering evidence to support their original impression and decision. It seems that many interviewers decide first and foremost which candidates they identify with, and adjust their interpretation of the answers to their questions, for example, to fit the type of person they identify with, who they want to appoint. A study in the *Journal of Occupational and Organisational Psychology* by Frieder *et al.* in 2015 explored how quickly it took job interviewers to come to a decision about a candidate. It indicated that 5% of them make their decision within the first few minutes, and almost 30% within five minutes.

Most interviewers, it seems, make decisions about hiring someone after five minutes. Over half (52%) make their decision within five to fifteen minutes of starting the interview, and only 22.5% make their mind up at the end.

So, if it's true that we choose our politicians based on their identities, and that many of us decide who we want to appoint for a job within fifteen minutes, then it raises concerns at all levels – not just regarding our choice of politicians, but also in the recruitment and decision-making process for taking on a new employee.

A person's performance and abilities are often irrelevant – it has more to do with identities and whether the person will fit into the institution; in the case of politicians, it has less to do with policies than identities, and whether we fit in with them. This makes it very difficult for anyone who is different to step into an interview room and be given a fair chance. Often their physical characteristics are immediately noticed by interviewers, some of whom then make decisions on the basis of whether they identify with the person or not. Worse still, some decisions are made about their suitability as early as the application stage, sometimes merely because the person's name is 'different'.

In my blog, I argued that inclusion has to be more than just normalising and fitting in. It's about belonging and being fully accepted and welcomed by any organisation or institution – about having a real seat at the table, being allowed to use one's full voice to make a real contribution. This means being given the time and space to value that voice and that contribution. This is an area in which organisations need support, to review their selection and recruitment processes.

They also need support to deal with allegations of racism, and to investigate complaints made by white junior staff against senior managers and leaders who happen to be black or from some minority ethnic group. In my experience, allegations like these are left unchallenged. Some HR departments are quick to put risk management above listening and dealing with such issues, or taking time to understand the lived experiences of black and minority ethnic managers. The result is negative outcomes for the managers which impact on their mental health. In 'First letter to white educational psychologists: We can't breathe – black Lives Matter' (2020), I wrote:

> *A focus is needed not only on the efficacy and applications of psychology in reducing disadvantage and removing barriers, but also on recruitment and selection processes and stereotypes and behaviours that impede the recruitment and progression of black and Asian minority ethnic psychologists within the profession.*

When we discriminate because of our prejudices and biases, we rob society of the potential benefits and contributions that these individuals may make. We reduce the much-needed diversity of thought in our teams and within boardrooms and – as McGhee (2021) reminded us – we all stand to lose out. The Six Stages Framework supports us to appreciate that we are all at different stages in a journey towards understanding and dealing with racism and promoting a more equitable society, which discourages (and aims to eliminate) discrimination according to race, colour, appearance, or other characteristics.

We need to be able to search for the 'gold' in others, rather than let the outside packaging (physical characteristics, culture, ethnicity, gender, work status or social standing) stop us from seeing and valuing them and their potential to contribute to society.

Creating safe spaces and allowing space for different voices is key to diversity of thought

In a blog dating from January 2021, I wrote about the importance of creating safe spaces and giving ethnic minorities the space to contribute to organisations. Here are some of my comments and observations.

I remember many occasions where I would raise my hand to make a contribution in a meeting only for the chair to ignore me and ask someone else to speak. When eventually I got an opportunity to speak, the time available was often half of that of other participants in the meeting. Some reading this may think, *you're just being sensitive, and how do you know it was because of your colour?* But when it happens time and time again it becomes an issue and – believe me – you know.

Many black and ethnic minorities tell similar stories of their experiences in meetings and not being given space to speak. The time made available in meetings for black and ethnic minorities is often cut short and this is part of the problem of non-inclusive organisations. True inclusion involves creating spaces where all voices can be heard and can make a contribution.

True inclusion starts with creating safe spaces, and this includes in meetings. We need to create spaces where *every* voice is heard and equal time is given for contributions. Chairs need to be supported to achieve this. Think how much richer discussions will be when we allow the space for new voices; when we create meeting spaces where we truly listen, value and hear different contributions. Diversity of thought increases, and organisations fully embrace inclusivity. Individual employees have a sense of belonging, safe in the knowledge that their contributions are valued and listened to, and they can make a difference to the organisation.

Sarah Fister Gale wrote an article in 2019 called 'Why diversity of thought is the key ingredient for better business'. She quoted Antonia Hock, the global head of the Ritz Carlton leadership centre, saying:

> *One of the reasons diverse companies are more successful on virtually every measure is that they bring multiple viewpoints to the table. Diverse teams have different life experiences, which causes individuals to approach problems differently, and to empathize with end-users in new ways. Hock says, 'The wider the diversity of experiences, the wider the pool of knowledge that the team will bring to each decision, idea or project'.*

Look around you today and ask yourself these questions:

- What is the make-up of my team or boardroom?

- Are we aware of what we are missing out on by not appointing managers and leaders using a values-based recruitment processes?
- Do we know what we *don't* know so we can challenge our thinking and no longer settle for the status quo – appointing people who reflect us and share our thinking no matter how ineffective or incompetent they are?
- Do we ensure fair treatment of black and other minority ethnic staff?
- Are we able to evaluate our efforts, measure performance and quality dimensions related to equality, diversity and inclusion?

How racism takes its toll on black and minority ethnic employees' mental health

Unfortunately my experiences in the workplace, which are shared by many other black and minority ethnic employees and senior managers, are that holding a management or senior leadership position can be difficult for many black and ethnic minorities. When they raise questions or challenge organisations or professional groups about systems that are biased and discriminate against them, the system finds ways to undermine their position and push them out – and HR processes can make it extremely difficult for them to get another job in the same position – if at all!

For many ethnic minorities, this just seems to be how the system works. My experience is that some organisations, including certain professional unions, commonly turn a blind eye. Individuals may be portrayed as an angry black/Asian-male stereotype, for example, and even worse for women. The organisations justify their actions and lack of inclusivity by saying: 'Well, they're difficult to work with' or 'They are aggressive' or 'If only they had phrased things differently, we would have listened'.

It is also evident that white junior staff often feel empowered to raise complaints about their managers from black or minority ethnic groups. The careers of many black and minority ethnic people have been damaged because senior managers failed to investigate their complaints or, worse still, because white senior leaders have colluded with the junior white complainants. It is important to recognise another real-world concern, people who see it as being too easy to play the 'race card' when things are not going as well as can be at work.

There was an incident in America recently in which a white woman phoned the police about a black man called Christian Cooper. Cooper had asked her to put her dog on a lead in a public park. However, she knew how much 'power' she wielded and threatened to call the police and tell them that he had threatened her; even though she was lying, she knew what the outcome would be.

Employers need to be aware of similar dynamics in the workplace, and ensure they have systems and processes for exploring them, in addition to a robust review of their complaints and investigation processes. In his article 'Moving beyond diversity toward racial equity', Ben Hecht (2020) stated:

Putting these skills into action at work requires deep understanding and harnessing power. Each of us is learning to ask 'What informal and formal power do I hold to shift culture? How should I wield it to change damaging norms and power dynamics within our institution?' For example, I long considered the departures of black staff members largely to be isolated cases. It took others in the organization to raise what I wasn't seeing: a pattern. That realization forced me to grapple with new questions, such as the racial competencies of those conducting exit interviews, what questions were being asked, and why the information gathered about those departures was not seriously interrogated.

The Six Stages Framework supports organisations in exploring the biases that exist, and in confronting their fears and engaging in conversations and processes that promote racial equity and inclusion. It helps organisations put individual welfare and mental health at the centre of the process, rather than focusing on merely protecting their organisation from negative publicity.

Training and up-skilling staff groups

In my experience, many organisations and professional groups (including psychologists) find it difficult to talk about racial equity and racism. During discussions on #dearwhitepsychologists (M'gadzah, 2020), I wondered what this apparent tendency for silence is all about – whether it's because of a fear of getting things wrong or because many psychologists are white and middle-class and do not see how the issues are important to them.

During a conversation with someone in my LinkedIn network, it was asserted that psychologists and other allied professionals should have no difficulty in supporting clients to deal with racism or its consequences, or the newly termed 'OCD-themed racism' (Williams, 2020), whereby some people with OCD (obsessive–compulsive disorder) are plagued by intrusive thoughts about racism. Some white people simply have difficulties dealing with racism and its implications. However, a large number of psychologists in another online group (#drshunguconversationsonrace) said they want more support and training for themselves because they still avoid exploring their beliefs on racism openly for fear of being judged.

As with unconscious bias, speaking about 'microaggressions' is challenging for many psychologists. It differs from the kind of trauma work they are used to, and many of them have yet to fully understand the concepts themselves before they can support others. There is plenty of support and training already on the disclosure of deeply traumatic experiences, including abuse of varying kinds, and psychologists and other therapists are well supported throughout their training and continuing professional development (CPD) to explore these issues and consider the relevant frameworks. Unfortunately, this is not the case for issues relating to racism, microaggression and unconscious bias.

For many people, merely talking about racial equity and racism is challenging and often confronting to the 'self'. DEI consultants and trainers are often better placed to deal with the issues, but they are unable to offer therapeutic support or the required conceptual frameworks.

I am not the only one to believe that training for psychology (and allied) professionals in this area needs to be prioritised and should be part of ongoing CPD. The work should include a review of the underpinning factors and theoretical frameworks that inform the psychology and our understanding of racism. It should also include the language we use to discuss racism.

The conversation has to start with psychologists becoming willing and able to engage in discussions on race; it is far more than simply publishing position statements and setting up working parties, task groups and finish groups. If psychologists and DEI consultants are to be successful in helping others deal with and understand racism and the trauma it causes, then the work has to start with the 'self'.

In her article 'The fight against racism must continue: Psychologists are looking inward to dismantle racism within the field', Zara Abrams (2021) reminds us of the work psychologists need to do:

> *In the midst of America's racial reckoning, psychologists are playing a key role in rethinking bias, policing, and other issues. But psychologists say the field itself has its own systemic injustices to dismantle. ... 'Many disciplines are looking inward right now, and we are no exception,' says Roberts. 'The idea is to review psychology, but not for the sake of tearing it down – for the sake of making it more equitable and inclusive'.*

Psychologists need to engage fully with these issues. Like other professionals, if we are to help others (and ourselves) we must first face all the issues ourselves, and this means being able to talk about racism and to support others to challenge it, while we lead the way.

I had the pleasure of speaking to Dani Saadu, Global Director of People Development at Collinson. I saw him on the BBC News talking about his father's legacy as an NHS consultant, and his story resonated with my memories of my late father who had also worked as a nurse in the NHS. He authored an article entitled 'How can we improve representation of black executives and non-executives in FTSE 100 companies?' Recent research shows that black representation at board level is non-existent. Why is this happening in the UK? And how can organisations change their approach to turn the dial on racially diverse leadership? Saadu informed us of the negative statistics in relation to top executive roles, describing how the figures are shocking and depressing:

> *I flicked on to Sky News to check the daily numbers of Covid cases and was presented with a report stating there were no black people in the top three roles – Chair, CEO, or CFO – in any of the FTSE 100 firms. Even more depressing is that the percentage of black people on the boards of FTSE 100 companies has gone down from 1.3% to 1.1% according to the Green Park Business Leaders 2021 index.*

He stated that a strong effective HR function is key and there is a need for honest conversations at senior-leadership level about the importance and benefits of diversity and inclusion. He wrote:

> *It would be easy to blame systemic racism but, in my experience, there is more going*

on here. There is a real lack of honest conversations being had at the most senior levels about the importance of diversity and inclusion and the benefits it brings. A lot of companies see D&I as a tick-box exercise and do not understand how it drives competitive advantage and contributes to more profits. ... There is still a lack of awareness, education and empathy when it comes to diversity and inclusion. From my experience, when D&I is discussed in the workplace, people tend to default to gender diversity rather than racial diversity. People feel more comfortable with discussing gender inequalities than race. ... In the multiple conversations I have had with leaders about the lack of racial diversity at senior levels, most people's default stance is to get defensive, or think that I am trying to push positive discrimination, or that I am calling their organisation racist. Once I have had the chance to explain properly where I am coming from as a black person who is very passionate about their career, a lot of people get it and actively try to support the diversity and inclusion agenda.

He also pointed us to some important questions to ask in this area, such as:

- Are we having enough challenging conversations about diversity and inclusion?
- Are we making time to raise awareness and educate the key decision-makers in the workplace?
- Are we creating positive environments to have these conversations?

As you can see, the need for challenging conversations resonates with the Six Stages Framework. In exploring how we can improve things, Saadu goes on to outline the need for open and honest conversations:

Until BAME people can have more open, honest conversations about racial diversity in the workplace with white people things will never improve. The conversations need to be focused on the problem and solutions, not on making it personal to individuals. ... Diversity and inclusion needs to be an official strategic priority for all companies in the UK and there should be clear SMART D&I targets or objectives that are shared publicly so that board members are held to account. All FTSE 100 companies should have a D&I role on the board and they should have good quality people data on D&I that should be measured on an ongoing basis.

While making it clear he does not believe in positive discrimination, Saadu explained that there are plenty of black people in the UK who are capable of being CEOs, Chairs and CFOs. He pointed to the lack of collaboration between internal talent management functions with their D&I function (that is, if a company has one), saying:

... therefore people from underrepresented groups do not get easily identified as talent.

I was struck by the similarities between our messages. Saadu highlighted the importance of talent management functions being critical to identifying and developing talent from the black community:

All talent management strategies should crossover with D&I strategies to ensure

> *people from all groups are getting equal opportunities. ... It is very important that senior HR professionals are having open honest conversations with their leaders about the importance of diversity and inclusion. When it comes to talent reviews and succession planning, good HR professionals should challenge their leaders if there is a lack of diversity in the people pipeline. It is critical for the HR function to encourage, support and drive positive action wherever possible.*

A new generation of leaders and understanding personality traits

I watched Dr Larry Richard (2021) talking about the seven outlier personality traits of lawyers and how they relate to innovation and leadership. Dr Richard, speaking about the importance of social interactions, explained that:

> *... there is research that came out in the last ten to twelve years that is very compelling and it tells us that social connection is one of the most single most important things that we can do for our well-being, for our longevity and for our overall life satisfaction. So, we really have to think do we want to continue trivialising this area like we have been doing.*

He spoke about the importance of cognitive empathy and taking the perspective of others. He explained that this can be taught and people can be supported to pay attention to other people. He highlighted the importance of resilience, social connections and having social interactions with others at an emotional, rather than cerebral, level. He also explored the traits that are needed by law firms to enable them to adapt to uncertainty and unprecedented change. In an ever-changing and adapting world, law firms need to attract more people who have different personality traits.

I wondered what personality traits are needed for psychologists and DEI consultants to promote work in the area of DEI and support these assessments and complex conversations. He spoke about leadership, the change process and how best to provide feedback, and talked about research showing criticism backfires and causes the hippocampus to shut down, thereby preventing people from learning; so the best thing to do is to be supportive, positive and reinforcing to bring out the best in people. The more you can do this, the more their performance and they are supported to adapt to change.

This resonates with messages in the Six Stages Framework; it is important, when providing feedback in the area of racial equity, to show compassion and avoid criticism and judgement of others to prevent them from shutting down and stop learning.

10

Diversity and inclusion in boardrooms

Values-based leadership

In considering racial equity and inclusion work, the importance of culture and values cannot be underestimated. But how can we promote a greater understanding of the role of values and culture to support organisations? It is important to identify the organisation's values, beliefs and cultural rules and the behaviours that we expect, then hold a mirror up to the staff to see whether they are living by them. Senior leaders and teams should and review their organisational values on a regular basis. They need to understand how these values relate to racial equity and inclusion work. Beliefs have to be grounded in fact, science and data.

In 2018, I co-wrote an article (M'gadzah and Poate-Joyner, 2018) entitled 'Psychologists on boards: promoting greater inclusion' about the timeliness of reaching out to boardrooms on DEI matters. It seemed important to highlight that the work should start at a senior-leadership level. This is because the issue is not just about skin colour or culture – it's about values too.

I'm often reminded by Umesh Prabhu that there are good and bad people in every racial group – that bullying and discrimination occurs within the same racial groups – and that representation is not the answer. It is important to keep this in mind when we endeavour to promote inclusivity. Values and an understanding of individual and organisational 'belief systems' must be at the forefront of every discussion.

In discussions between executives of Fortune 500 companies and Ben Hecht (2020), the CEO of Living Cities, Hecht outlined three of the most important lessons in the journey towards building and maintaining a racial equity culture. These are to:

- understand how power works and use it for change
- understand and embrace conflict as part of the process
- commit to ongoing learning and long-term transformation.

As he stated, in order to:

> *... build a new, more inclusive culture, we first needed to be able to see the norms, values, and practices in our institutions that advantage white people and ways of working, to the exclusion and oppression of all others. To do this, we had to commit time and resources to staff members' individual learning. Understanding history,*

interrogating personal biases, building empathy and respect for others, getting comfortable with vulnerability – these skills require training and ongoing practice. This is dedicated, individual work that must be modelled from the top.

He reflected on the impact of not doing this work and failing to make changes to the organisational culture and norms:

If no one had challenged me on the turnover patterns of black staff, we likely never would have changed our behaviors. Similarly, it is risky and uncomfortable to point out racist dynamics when they show up in daily interactions, such as the treatment of people of color in meetings, or team or work assignments. ... The cultures we seek to create cannot brush past or ignore conflict, or worse, direct blame or anger toward those who are pushing for needed transformation. ... My job as a leader continuously is to model a culture that is supportive of that conflict by intentionally setting aside defensiveness in favor of public displays of vulnerability when disparities and concerns are raised.

The Six Stages Framework recognises the importance of research and evidence-based practice. It is involved in collaborative ongoing research that seeks to establish best practices in DEI and efficacy of the DEI strategy. The research seeks to understand the efficacy of organisational equity, diversity and inclusion policies by exploring a best-practice approach to strategic policy development. It considers various factors as measures of success with respect to impacts on adoption of the strategies, including:

- completion of a comprehensive workplace assessment
- a clearly defined policy in place with clear objectives
- an equity analysis strategy as part of the policy framework
- a sound accountability mechanism
- a learning, development and communication strategy as part of the policy framework.

Board-level diversity

While some people do not recognise the need for anti-racism training, it is something that should be considered at all levels. It seems especially vital for eliciting change in organisations. I decided to make the issue of racism 'my business' and not turn away from it.

In 2020, I was involved in discussions with the late David Doughty on diversity and inclusion. When I visited his website, NED (Non-Executive Directors) Works, I noticed the lack of programmes focusing on boardroom diversity, so I decided to approach him with an outline of a course I had designed. As a result, we agreed to work together and set up a LinkedIn page on diversity and inclusion in the boardroom, to deliver training to boards and provide free webinars for those looking to get their first board role.

While I was preparing the material for our first course, *Diversity and Inclusion in the Boardroom* (in collaboration with NED Works, Excellencia Limited and Evolve Leadteam Ltd), I realised even more just how important it is to focus on diversity, equity and inclusion at senior-management and leadership levels. Events around the world were now shining light on organisations' responses to diversity and inclusion, especially the death of George Floyd. My colleague and I wrote in our article (M'gadzah and Poate-Joyner, 2018):

> *The time has never been more right for boards of charities, services and organisations to engage in conversations around diversity and inclusion, exploring the benefits of, and the barriers to inclusion. It appears to be an urgent need to explore to assist boards to achieve greater participation from diverse and under-represented groups of people.*

This is still the case today, three years later (at the time of writing), because change in this area has been slow (Charity Commission, 2020; Hampton–Alexander Review, 2021). However, there does seem to have been a shift as many more organisations realise the need to address diversity and inclusion issues.

I remember David Doughty reminding me that my ideas on DEI and boardrooms may well be ahead of the curve and encouraging me to keep going. We collaborated as long as we could and I am sad he was not able to see our work to completion. I hope that one day I will be able to look back and say we are no longer ahead of the curve.

Why should board members use the Six Stages Framework?

Racism is about power. For true change to take place in society, the interventions must be at structural and institutional levels. The *Diversity and Inclusion in the Boardroom* course is critical for boards that want to promote greater inclusivity in their organisations. It takes board members through the first steps in exploring how their board functions and where it is in the processes of fostering inclusivity and facilitating change, while supporting and challenging its values, beliefs and behaviours in relation to racial differences. The following questions were posed to participants of a *Diversity and Inclusion in the Boardroom* webinar in February 2021:

- What does your board need to do to make it more diverse and inclusive?
- Is your company board or charity board as diverse and inclusive as it could be?
- Are your committees and meetings addressing issues of racial equity and inclusion?
- Is it safe to do so?
- What are your board's key challenges?
- What makes your board a safe place?

The 2017 research report, *Taken on Trust*, published by the Charity Commission found that 92% of trustees are white, 51% are retired, 75% are richer than average, and 60% have a professional qualification. In 2020, the UK's Charity Commission published an updated version of the Charity Governance Code, with revised recommendations on DEI and ethics, and highlighting the importance of work in this area. It is essential reading for all chairs and trustees of charities:

> *These improvements to the Charity Governance Code reflect changes in society and the broader context in which charities are working. The updated Code is designed to help charities adopt good practice and secure better outcomes for the communities they serve. We know that charities are at varying stages in their efforts to fully adopt the Code, including achieving equality of opportunity, diversity and inclusion, and the updated Code is designed to help charities on this journey. We've also heard that charities and boards would like more guidance on how to improve their approach to DEI. In response, we are asking charity umbrella and infrastructure bodies to provide more guidance and support to charities, to help them meet the recommended practice in the Code.*

The Hampton-Alexander Review of 2021 indicated that making changes at board level is a slow process. British boardrooms are no longer the 'exclusive men's clubs' they used to be; now there are no male-only boardrooms in the FTSE350. Men still dominate the upper ranks of firms, but the number of women on these boards has increased by 50% over the last five years. Early in 2021, I was talking on LinkedIn to Nicholas Cheffings, previously a partner in and Global Chair of Hogan Lovells law firm and now senior counsel at Hogan Lovells who carries out advocacy work on diversity, inclusion, anti-racism, equity and equality in business and society. In response to my question on supporting boards to be more inclusive, he said:

> *Boards need to first recognise the benefits of diversity and inclusion and they have to want to change.*

In my view, boards come across many challenges and barriers to DEI, including:

- psychological factors
- cultural factors
- functional factors
- financial factors.

In the webinar mentioned above, I explored the DEI challenges facing boards and diversity at board level. The key challenges seem to be in four main areas: psychological, cultural, functional and financial. Around 70% of the participants considered psychological factors to be the main barrier.

In considering such challenges, it's important to explore each organisation's or board's unique story; it is also important to explore the payoffs (whether conscious or unconscious) for the board: what does the board gain by not changing? *Table 1* (overpage) lists some of these common challenges, along with possible justifications and payoffs.

The Six Stages Framework helps organisations review their priorities in the area of DEI. As part of the Board Diversity programme, Inclusion Psychologists Ltd supports these priorities using the framework to identify where individuals or organisations are in terms of their level of understanding about racism and their ability to deal with it. Following the assessment, Inclusion Psychologists Ltd identifies a baseline in terms of organisational priorities and sets targets and outcomes for specific teams or the whole organisation. The framework helps individuals, teams and organisations to achieve these priorities and outcomes, with a focus on sustainability within the organisation. There are many DEI challenges and barriers that boards are faced with.

Commitment to change in boardrooms starts with senior leaders

Senior leaders need to find ways of 'building bridges of empathy' in order to bring different communities together, foster a sense of belonging and shift away from narratives of blame and racial intolerance. For real change to occur, it requires real commitment at both individual and organisational levels. This starts by having conversations about race and speaking up, with honest conversations about personal experiences of differences regardless of one's own race. There must be an understanding of emotional intelligence and an openness to explore the principles of empathy, compassion and belonging. The real work in achieving change can then begin!

The Diversity and Inclusion in the Boardroom course is the first step in raising awareness and admitting that organisations do not always 'get it right' and need to do things differently. This involves challenging existing cultural norms and beliefs as well as any biases and prejudices that disadvantage ethnic minority groups. A failure to act leads to more incidents like the storming of the US Capitol and nurtures a society that is intolerant of difference, in which ordinary people can be radicalised by extremist groups who feel entitled by the colour of their skin and will stop at nothing to snatch power away from others. Failure to act can also lead to disenfranchised groups who feel like they have no place in society and do not belong because of their racial and ethnic background, taking whatever steps they see as corrective action. Either way, the result may be an even greater polarisation of society – one in which individuals are vulnerable to manipulation or radicalisation, feeding on their fears and with the promise of a better life.

In June 2021, we saw a range of initiatives aimed at increasing diversity within the boardroom. Perkins Coie partners, James Williams and Stewart Landefeld were named as co-leaders of the Black Boardroom Initiative, which is making efforts to increase the diversity of S&P 500 corporate boards. Lisa Stiffler (2021) reported that they aim to do this by:

> *... training cohorts of potential candidates. Its goal is to increase the number of Black leaders on public boards to one in eight by 2028 – a ratio that matches the fraction of America's Black population. Right now, Black board members are approximately one in 24.*

In her article entitled 'The room where it happens – where leadership inclusion begins', Teresa Hopke (2021) stated that:

> *Inclusive leadership begins in the room where it happens. And when it doesn't, it sets an organization up for an inevitable and embarrassing fall.*

Table 1: Key challenges facing boards in implementing diversity and inclusion.

Domain	Typical stances	Justification (the board's story)	Payoffs
PSYCHOLOGICAL	Gravitate towards sameness Fear of change Fear of differences	Unconscious bias Conscious bias	Belonging Comfort Acceptance
CULTURAL	"This is the way we have always done things." Ideologies and beliefs Unspoken codes Predictability and ease	"These people will not fit in." "We value different things." "It's what we are used to."	
FUNCTIONAL	Qualifications Socioeconomic status Board-speak Experience	"We have always had accountants or finance experts on the board." "Newcomers will not understand how our board functions." "There are no women or ethnic minorities with this level of skill or expertise."	
FINANCIAL	"Financial constraints stop us making the changes we want to."	"If only we had the money, we would make the changes needed in this area."	Staying the same Comfort
OTHER	Unspecified	"There are many reasons we cannot make the changes. It's difficult to explain – you have to understand our board's story and journey."	

She described how organisations should not wait until there is public outrage over a lack of inclusive leadership to inspire them to inventory their own practices. She reminded us:

> *Companies that are diligently developing a culture of inclusivity will outperform, outpace, out-shine, and outwit those who don't",*

And she quoted Vernā Myers, Vice President of Inclusion Strategy (Netflix) thus:

> *Be consciously inclusive. Inclusive leaders create environments where people of all backgrounds feel respected, can contribute their talent and perspectives, and are given fair access to meaningful opportunity. Most of us think of ourselves as kind, fair, and well-meaning, and we are, but being well-meaning is not enough when it comes to being an Inclusive Leader.*

Reflections from conversations in the EverydayCHPsychology Clubhouse rooms: Praise for the Six Stages Framework

In March 2021 I was introduced to the Clubhouse Social Audio app of Tatenda Mutsvairo, an entrepreneur, business consultant and project manager, whose app enables hosting of live discussions and provides opportunities for participating through speaking and listening.

I host discussions within the EverydayCHPsychology and Six Stages Framework Clubhouses, and am supported by a number of colleagues who help me moderate the rooms. One of these rooms focuses on opening up conversations on race and is called the prejudice–racism spectrum, and it is here that I have introduced the concepts of the Six Stages Framework, bridges of empathy, caves of privilege and the prejudice–racism spectrum. Below are some comments and reflections from people who have attended our Clubhouse rooms (July–August 2021) and what they say about us and their reflections on our conversations:

> *Yesterday I joined Dr Shungu Hilda M'gadzah's chatroom in the Clubhouse. What an uplifting experience ... please do yourself a favour and join one of her debates. The discussion was on mentoring and being a mentor. It's a subject close to my heart and our debate helped to confirm and develop many of my thoughts on the subject. My first time on Clubhouse as well – shout out to the platform ... amazing! Please join the next debate –you will not regret it.*
> Nicoline Kakora-Shiner, Independent Clinical Trainer

> *These conversations couldn't be more relevant – can't wait to hear Dr Shungu Hilda M'gadzah explore this on Clubhouse.*
> Sally Casterton, Director, Garner Financial Solutions Ltd

> *An absolute delight to join Dr Shungu on #6stages in her Clubhouse room today. Discussing the definitions of racism. Join her weekly Clubhouse room, in a safe space, where you can discuss topics that facilitate growth and knowledge.*
> Kay Simpson, Integrative Counsellor Private Practice MBACP

It is always a struggle being different in any community. You really feel left out and somewhat alone dealing with discrimination. Growing up a queer person I have always felt the need to voice my opinion louder and try not to be overshadowed or silenced, always ask for my rights and fight for my life. Discrimination against anything that doesn't go with what so called – society norms – is an ideology that we really need to shed light on more, and speak louder about the issues that we have, and try to detach ourselves as human beings from being judgemental and having negative feelings towards anything that we don't understand. We as humans need to open up, be less oblivious to what happens around us, and listen. We need compassion in our lives in order to create a safe environment and space for everyone so we can evolve. We should not have to restrict free speech – give people a chance to voice their concerns and feelings. Education is very important; people are not born with hate, but they gain it from their toxic environment. Hence why we need to educate people in order to create a safer environment for everyone.
Hassan Sahib, Founder of Qadeera

Racism is such a hateful reality. Hatred breeds hatred. And as we all know, hatred is built on the pedestal of fear. We all understand fear as a basic human emotion and that it is a learned response. This learned response explains not only the behavior of the oppressor, but it also explains why the oppressed often finds it difficult to empathise with his/ her oppressor. It is because of this that we can also say that fear breeds fear. And that is what prevents us from being able to empathize. The point of empathizing is not to change the other person but to build bridges of understanding across the river of fear. Until such time that either side gets over his/her personal apprehensions, we will not see an end to the unfortunate human phenomenon of racism. For it is only through the building of bridges that we can come to see truth that we all fall within a spectrum of biases, prejudices, and – yes – racism. And realizing that is a good thing because it places both sides on common ground. Acknowledging that fact or at the very least, accommodating the notion is a bitter pill that we all might need to swallow but it may also well be the cure to this social disease.
Mike Doria, Advocate for Values Development

As far as the discussion went, we had some really interesting input from participants from the Middle East. They shared the experiences that they had grown up in Middle Eastern countries. We had contributions shared from the perspectives of people who identify as Black Arabs and/or members of the LGBTQIA+ community. It was a really rich discussion, and a common theme was that of the power of allyship across different group.
Marie Odhiambo, Honorary Assistant Psychologist at Inclusion Psychologists Limited, Psychology HBSc Candidate and Sociology Research Assistant at University of Toronto

This has been an amazing conversation led by Dr Shungu Hilda M'gadzah, with amazing insights from Sally Casterton, Marie Odhiambo and Tatenda M. I learned so much and hopefully added some value to. What a beautiful set of open-hearted

explorers seeking to truly support understanding and equity. Some of my major takeaways are: It is always important for white allies to speak up about topics of inequity and inequality. The key differences between performative messaging and meaningful action are intention and authenticity. I have been known to be 'noisy' on social media in the past and I think when that happens it is due to the wrong energy (from me). Doing inner work, checking our beliefs, questioning why one may wrap up so much identity and self-worth in a football team. The importance of self-awareness and checking biases are some example explorations that may be helpful. Education starts at home; what language do you use with your partners and families? What tone and intention is being shared with talking about others that are 'different' to you? Do give Shungu and her #clubhouse room a follow, and I am very curious to be in further dialogue around these topics with people that may be interested, especially in Shungu's rooms, or in my systemic leadership room.
Garry Turner, Strategic Advisor

I appreciate this framework and what it offers us – the opportunity to be curious about our internalized racism and be empathetic of others. When we view racism on a spectrum, rather than as a binary choice, we have more room for learning and curiosity.
Nina Simonds, Leadership Facilitator and Executive Coach

In July 2021, following the post by Nicholas Cheffings (past Global Chair of Hogan Lovells) in which he condemned racist abuse, Gary Turner posted this:

Powerful from Nicholas Cheffings, so appreciate this. ... Our CH chat this week and some other dialogues have been very clarifying after the past week's events.

Here is a selection of the comments that followed:

I believe that the concept of understanding racism–prejudice as existing on a spectrum is not only innovative but worth further exploration. The discourse surrounding racism and prejudice is an inevitable and uncomfortable one. It is often met with avoidance, denial and defensiveness, resulting in many conversations not going further than surface level. However, once people are willing to dive deeper into the conversation, and themselves, valuable strides are made. The conversations had within the Everyday Club House Psychology room on Clubhouse, regarding race, have recently been centred on the different definitions/conceptualizations of racism (mostly related to power dynamics). Within that discussion is the notion of racism/prejudice being best understood as existing on a spectrum, rather than more traditional black and white, concrete definitions. Racism is not just one thing, rather it rears its ugly head in various ways across time and place. By widening the definition of racism and prejudice, I believe that people are able to introspect on their own views, beliefs and biases (which we all have to some extent). Through the idea of everyone existing somewhere on this spectrum, we are able to move away from the idea that 'I do not do X, therefore I am not racist'. Instead, a shift in thinking might lead us to say, 'I might not do X, but

sometimes I believe/act like Y, so maybe I am contributing to the ways in which racism manifests and affects people'. Discussing racism and prejudice is never going to be a comfortable task, nor should it be. But maybe if we change the way we approach the discussion, and instead centre the desire to further learn and understand both the topic, and our own contributions/views to it, we can make significant steps to change.
Marie Odhiambo, Honorary Assistant Psychologist at Inclusion Psychologists Limited, Psychology HBSc Candidate and Sociology Research Assistant at University of Toronto

Shining a light on the racism spectrum to define and establish it will enable its use in educating our society, especially where individuals do not acknowledge their racist behaviour. Racism is complex because although for many it's not experienced as it was in the 'Apartide' [sic] era it is certainly still active in its subtle forms within Societal Systems, the community and in the mind of individuals whose idea of white privilege, is just their way of life. A well-defined racism spectrum covering the range could be a useful educational tool now, especially for the younger upcoming generation. So that their future may be racist free, this is my hope.
Dina O'Ketch, Founder of Well-being Monitor

It seems to me that every successful person out there has had a mentor or many mentors in their lives. Someone to provide guidance, support, or a trusted sounding board; providing space for candid dialogue is such an important aspect of personal development. In a competitive world, where as individuals we are racing to achieve our goals, we can get caught up in the mesh of daily 'must do's', so it is refreshing to be seen and validated by a mentor. Being seen, validated, acknowledged makes all the hard work seem worthwhile and inspires the drive to carry on.
Dina O'Ketch, Founder of Well-being Monitor

Concluding comments

In this book I have set out some of the issues related to present-day racism. As Sarah Lacey, a secondary school teacher, once said when I asked her to review an earlier version of the book:

> *Dr M'gadzah tackles head-on the issues of modern-day racism. The book is set within the difficult, turbulent and often unsettling world of today. The book inspires interest by referring to current affair issues, such as the tragic death of George Floyd, the Black Lives Matter movement, and the Harry and Meghan interview with Oprah Winfrey. By using popular cultural references, such as The Color Purple (by Alice Walker), Dr M'gadzah engages the reader. The Six Stage framework promotes optimism and empathy at a time of great need.*

Aishling Dempsey, an MSc Clinical Health Psychology student and Psychology Assistant at Inclusion Psychologists Ltd, stated:

> *I have just finished reading through your book and I am truly blown away. It was refreshing, thoughtful and inspiring. Reading in detail the conceptualisation of the framework and its positioning in everyday life as a tool was very interesting. The Six Stages Framework is an action-based positive tool that will speak to many people and provide the language many people feel that they don't have to speak about their own biases and racism. "What is special about the Six Stages Framework, is that it is a positive, action-based, non-judgemental tool that is essential to addressing sensitive topics.*

I certainly hope I have managed to engage you in the same way that I engaged Sarah Lacey and Aishling Dempsey. More than that, I hope my messages have been clear. Racism is everybody's business. It affects us all, and how we all deal with it will determine how we all manage to live peacefully together on this planet. We can either choose to do the work and promote our understanding of and ability to deal with racism – taking us upwards on the positive trajectory of the Six Stages Framework – or we can choose to ignore and deny the experiences of the countless people who are affected by racism on a daily basis– taking us down the negative trajectory, into a world where none of us are safe.

Either way, the actions we take have real consequences – not just for ourselves or our friends and families, but for humanity as a whole and for future generations. We need to recognise the role that each of us has in ensuring that we successfully tackle acts of bias, discrimination and racism, and that we speak up when we can. We all share the responsibility for creating a world in which it is not okay to kneel on someone's neck and treat them as if they are less than human because of the colour of their skin. We must all play our part in sending out clear messages and appropriate responses when we witness discrimination of any kind – including racism. We cannot turn the other way in the hope that racism will magically disappear, nor can we think that segregation or keeping ourselves separate will solve these issues.

Everyone should play a part in eradicating racism – but it is a matter of choice and willingness to engage with the issues. Which path do you choose? The one which that takes you further down the negative trajectory of the framework, or the one which that will take you on the positive axis, to deepen your understanding of racial issues? We must all be willing to do the work and the learning and to upskill ourselves, to challenge racism and create better leaders for today, tomorrow and the future – leaders who will be allies and who will champion racial harmony.

We all need a world in which we all embrace differences and diversity, and work and live together peacefully, side by side, without fear – a world in which we build 'bridges of empathy' and stand up for each other. In such a world we will all benefit. And our efforts will have an impact on our homes, schools, colleges, universities, businesses and workplaces. So all of us has to do the work and engage in conscious inclusion education or training programmes, willing to engage in conversations to explore the myriad issues and further develop our understanding.

When future generations ask, "What did you do to try and create more harmony on this planet?", what will your answer be?

Perhaps the racial reckoning we have seen really is a new beginning, and perhaps the current global momentum will propel us all into action – hopefully with tangible results – and maybe this time things will be different. Perhaps we will all 'be able to breathe', and perhaps young black and minority ethnic people will not have to suffer discrimination and racism in the same way that so many have.

There are signs that things are changing, albeit slowly. Some organisations are taking the right steps to shift cultures and achieve the changes that are required. We've witnessed some notable events, the sentencing of Derek Chauvin for the murder of George Floyd and an increasing number of people being held accountable for their actions. These are small steps, certainly, but they are steps in the right direction.

So we must all play our part and continue to help keep the diversity wheels turning, to bring about real systemic change, and policy and practice changes, and new legislation and reform wherever it's needed.

References and further reading

Abrams, Z. (2021) The fight against racism must continue: Psychologists are looking inward to dismantle racism within the field. *American Psychological Society* 52(1). Available at: https://www.apa.org/monitor/2021/01/trends-fight-racism

Adams, J. (2021) *Naomi Osaka explores mental health and the media's scrutiny.* Available at: https://www.colorlines.com/articles/naomi-osaka-explores-mental-health-and-medias-scrutiny (accessed August 2021).

Agarwal, P. (2020) *It's the perfect time to stop our unconscious bias going viral.* Available at: https://www.theguardian.com/lifeandstyle/2020/apr/12/its-the-perfect-time-to-stop-our-unconscious-bias-going-viral (accessed August 2021) (accessed August 2021).

Agarwal, P. (2020) *Sway: Unravelling Unconscious Bias.* Bloomsbury Sigma.

Ajayi, L. (2018) *Why we need to callout casual racism.* Available at: https://ideas.ted.com/why-we-need-to-call-out-casual-racism/ (accessed August 2021).

Alibhai-Brown, Y. (2020) *Racism is not just a white problem – it's time we Asians confronted our own prejudices.* Available at: https://inews.co.uk/news/long-reads/racism-south-asian-prejudices-black-lives-matter-753885 (accessed August 2021).

Amaechi J. (2020) *Privilege blinds us to plight of others who lack it.* Available at: https://www.ft.com/content/e394fd7b-5bdb-4d96-8375-a10a24e960c2 (accessed August 2021).

Amaechi, J. (2021) Twitter post. Available at: https://twitter.com/JohnAmaechi (accessed August 2021).

Amaechi, J. (2021) *Our experiences are not a myth: John Amaechi's rousing reaction to UK's race report.* Available at: https://www.lbc.co.uk/radio/presenters/david-lammy/john-amaechi-rousing-reaction-to-uks-diversity-race-report/ (accessed August 2021).

Beckwith, M. (2021) https://en.wikipedia.org/wiki/Michael_Beckwith (accessed August 2021).

Bennett, M.J. (2007) *Social justice and intercultural development: new views on campus intergroup relations.* Available at: https://www.idrinstitute.org/wp-content/uploads/2018/02/social_justice_ic_development.pdf (accessed August 2021).

Black, D. (2021) *The Capitol attack was White supremacy, plain and simple.* Available at: https://edition.cnn.com/2021/01/10/opinions/capitol-attack-white-supremacy-daniel-black/index.html (accessed August 2021).

Blackman, M. (2001) *Noughts and Crosses.* Random House.

Bolton, T., M'gadzah, S. H. (1999) Challenging inequality in educational psychology practice: perceptons of educational psychologists in training and current practice in London educational psychology services. The British Psychological Society: Challenging racism and inequality in education and child psychology. *Educational and Child Psychology* 16(3). Available at: https://shop.bps.org.uk/educational-child-psychology-vol-6-no-3-1999-challenging-racism-and-inequality-in-education-and (accessed in August 2021).

Boscardin, C.K. (2015) Reducing implicit bias through curricular interventions. *Journal of General Internal Medicine* 30(12), 1726–28. Available at: https://www.ncbi.nlm.nih.gov/pmc/articles/PMC4636582/ (accessed August 2021).

Butler, P. (2021). *Barnardo's blogpost on white privilege did not breach charity laws. Charities regulator says post deemed 'ideological dogma' by Tory MPs was in line with the Barnardo's mission.* Available at: https://www.theguardian.com/world/2021/aug/04/barnados-blogpost-on-white-privilege-did-not-breach-charity-laws (accessed in August 2021).

Casterton, S. (2021) *Reflections on a Clubhouse Conversation – Statements condemning racism are not enough on their own, but what can we do as individuals.* Available at: https://www.linkedin.com/posts/sally-casterton-%F0%9F%8F%B3%EF%B8%8F%E2%80%8D%F0%9F%8C%88-46a5b235_talkandvalue-psychvalue-talktodrshungum-activity-6823233336236879872-62wi (accessed August 2021).

Chang, E.H., Milkman, K.L, Gromet, D. *et al.* (2019) *The mixed effects of online diversity training.* Available at: https://www.pnas.org/content/116/16/7778 (accessed August 2021).

Charity Commission (2017) *Taken on trust: the awareness and effectiveness of charity trusts in England and Wales.* Available at: https://assets.publishing.service.gov.uk/government/uploads/system/uploads/attachment_data/file/658766/20171113_Taken_on_Trust_awareness_and_effectiveness_of_charity_trustees.pdf (accessed August 2021).

Charity Commission (2020) *The Charity Governance Code.* Available at: https://www.charitygovernancecode.org/en/pdf (accessed August 2021).

Chenault, K. (2021) *Why companies must stand up for the right to vote.* Available at: https://edition.cnn.com/videos/tv/2021/04/04/exp-ip-chenault.cnn/video/playlists/inside-politics-highlights/. (accessed August 2021).

City Mental Health Alliance (2021) *Mental Health in the Workplace Toolkit: A toolkit to help businesses support the positive mental health of their people who are black or from a minority ethnic background.* Available at: https://citymha.org.uk. (accessed August 2021).

Commission on Race and Ethnic Disparities (2021) *The Report April 2021.* Available at: https://assets.publishing.service.gov.uk/government/uploads/system/uploads/attachment_data/file/974507/20210331_-_CRED_Report_-_FINAL_-_Web_Accessible.pdf (accessed August 2021).

Delgaudio, D. (2021) *Amoralman.* Alfred A. Knopf Publications.

Dempsey, A., M'gadzah, S.H.,Watson, S (awaiting publication) Diversity and racism in higher education: the Six Stages Framework. In: Meletiadou, E. (ed.) *Handbook of Research on Practices for Advancing Diversity and Inclusion in Higher Education.* IGI Global.

Dixon, A. (2011) *Can empathy reduce racism? A new study suggests we can keep our prejudices in check by trying to see the world through someone else's eyes.* Available at: https://greatergood.berkeley.edu/article/item/empathy_reduces_racism (accessed August 2021).

Equality Act (2010) Available at: https://www.legislation.gov.uk/ukpga/2010/15/contents (accessed August 2021).

Equality Human Rights Commission (2018) *Unconscious-bias training: an assessment of the evidence for effectiveness.* Available at: https://www.equalityhumanrights.com/sites/default/files/research-report-113-unconcious-bais-training-an-assessment-of-the-evidence-for-effectiveness-pdf.pdf (accessed August 2021).

Etutu, J., Shearing, H. (2021) *Meghan and Harry: Their experiences are not shocking to us.* Available on: https://www.bbc.co.uk/news/uk-56338476 (accessed August 2021).

Excellencia (2021) *Diversity and Inclusion in the Boardroom Webinar.* Available at: https://excellencia.co.uk/courses/course-registration/?action=evregister&event_id=202 (accessed August 2021).

Fister, G. (2019) *Why diversity of thought is the key ingredient for better business.* Available at: https://www.americanexpress.com/en-us/business/trends-and-insights/articles/why-diversity-of-thought-is-the-key-ingredient-for-better-business/ (accessed August 2021).

Fitzgerald, J. (2021) *How tennis, golf, and white anxiety block racial integration.* Available at: https://hbswk.hbs.edu/item/how-tennis-golf-and-white-anxiety-block-racial-integration?cid=spmailing-33415888-WK%20Newsletter%206-9-2021%20(1)-June%2009,%202021 (accessed August 2021).

Frieder, R., Van Iddekinge, C.H., Raymark, P. (2015) How quickly do interviewers reach decisions? An examination of interviewers' decision-making time across applicants. *Journal of Occupational and Organisational Psychology* 89(2), 223–248. Available at: https://bpspsychub.onlinelibrary.wiley.com/action/doSearch?ContribAuthorStored=Frieder%2C+Rachel+E (accessed August 2021).

Ginsburg, R.B. (1972) *Harvard community reflects on the life achievements of Ruth Bader Ginsburg.* Available at: https://news.harvard.edu/gazette/story/2020/09/harvard-community-reflects-on-the-life-achievements-of-ruth-bader-ginsburg/ (accessed August 2021).

Ginsburg, R.B. (1993) *The Supreme Court: Transcript of President's announcement and Judge Ginsburg's remarks.* Available at: https://www.nytimes.com/1993/06/15/us/supreme-court-transcript-presidents-announcement-judge-ginsburg-s-remarks.html (accessed August 2021).

Giordano, C. (2021) *Buckingham Palace considers appointing 'diversity chief': Royal family 'accept more needs to be done', source says.* Available at: https://www.independent.co.uk/news/uk/home-news/buckingham-palace-diversity-chief-racism-meghan-b1820320.html#comments (accessed August 2021).

Goleman, D. (2004) *Emotional Intelligence: Why it can Matter more than IQ.* Bloomsbury.

Government Green Paper (2017) *Children and Young People's Mental Health: Role of Education. House of Commons Education and Health Committees First Joint Report of the Education and Health Committees 2016–17.* Available at: https://www.publications.parliament.uk/pa/cm201617/cmselect/cmhealth/849/849.pdf (accessed August 2021).

Grossman, A. (2021) *Study of 1940 census reveals white boys who lived next door to black neighbors were more likely to become Democrats, growing into more liberal-minded adults after being exposed to people of different backgrounds.* Available at: https://www.dailymail.co.uk/news/article-9679537/White-boys-grew-one-door-black-neighbor-likely-Democrats.html (accessed August 2021).

Gunn, R. and Bortolotti, L. (2018) *Can delusions play a protective wrong?* Available at: https://link.springer.com/article/10.1007/s11097-017-9555-6 (accessed August 2021).

Gutoskey, E. (2020) *What's the difference between equity and equality? Mental floss.* Available at: https://www.mentalfloss.com/article/625404/equity-vs-equality-what-is-the-difference (accessed August 2021).

Haley, A. (1976) *Roots.* Doubleday.

Hammer, M. (2019) *The Intercultural Development Continuum (IDC™).* Available at: https://idiinventory.com/generalinformation/the-intercultural-development-continuum-idc/ (accessed August 2021).

Hampton–Alexander Review (2021) *FTSE Women Leaders (Press Release).* Avail-able at: https://ftsewomenleaders.com/wp-content/uploads/2021/02/Hampton-Alexander-Review-Press-Notice_24-Feb-2021.pdf (accessed August 2021).

Hampton–Alexander Review (2021) *Improving gender balance. Five-year summary report.* Available at: https://ftsewomenleaders.com/wp-content/uploads/2021/02/HA-REPORT-2021_FINAL.pdf (accessed August 2021).

Hand, J. and Green, J. (2021) *Diversity matters/delivers/wins revisited in S&P 500® firms.* Cited in: Todd, S. (2021) *Is McKinsey wrong about the financial benefits of diversity?* Available at: https://qz.com/work/2038103/is-mckinsey-wrong-about-the-financial-benefits-of-diversity/?utm_source=email&utm_medium=quartz-at-work&utm_content=0d522257-f4a6-11eb-8191-2af58326e3c5&fbclid=IwAR32GgZn9eEvdMGVLw80gk8BW39GzKjnjIl5uUofknbjAionXgcaXjJKOMY (accessed August 2021).

Harley-McKeown, L. (2021) *Racial discrimination still rife in UK businesses, study finds.* Available at: https://uk.finance.yahoo.com/news/diversity-inclusion-discrimination-workplace-henley-business-school-research-230125671.html?guccounter=1&gucereferrer=aHR0cHM6Ly90LmNvL0J0dENUSVVPR3E_YW1wPTE&guce_referrer_sig=AQAAAKe2PMck8U7TOdlLRV3pZM4-iEfuwQWPB5NNg89q9JdA0BCA9y_mGqszq3N7vnoxt4NUSRyfobZkjZVDA_dtxwzzASu96HejVb3Vn78jNtP_S8wleCsSJs8jWt1aX8RE1avtZivUiwSEXQLwP6rti3GSl8VQWdQ9efUdCFfB1Lx (accessed August 2021).

Hecht, B. (2020) *Moving Beyond Diversity Toward Racial Equity.* Available at: https://hbr.org/2020/06/moving-beyond-diversity-toward-racial-equity (accessed August 2021).

Hemmings, C. (2017) *Be a Man and How Macho Culture Damages Us and How to Escape It.* Biteback Publishing.

Hirsch, A. (2018) *Brit(ish): On Race, Identity and Belonging.* Jonathan Cape.

Hock, A. (2019) *Why diversity of thought is the key ingredient for better business.* Available at: https://www.americanexpress.com/en-us/business/trends-and-insights/articles/why-diversity-of-thought-is-the-key-ingredient-for-better-business/ (accessed August 2021).

Hollon, S., Kendall, P. (1980) Cognitive self-statements in depression: development of an automatic thoughts questionnaire. *Cognitive Therapy and Research* 4(4), 383–395. doi:10.1007/bf01178214 (accessed August 2021).

Hood, L. (2021) *The Conversation. Learning about white privilege isn't harmful to white working-class children – viewpoint.* Available at: https://theconversation.com/learning-about-white-privilege-isnt-harmful-to-white-working-class-children-viewpoint-163390 (accessed August 2021).

Hopke, T. (2021) *The room where it happens – where leadership inclusion begins.* Available at: https://www.forbes.com/sites/teresahopke/2021/05/24/the-room-where-it-happens-where-leadership-inclusion-begins/ (accessed August 2021).

Hopkinson, J. (2020) *Racism and the misconceptions surrounding it.* Available at: https://www.hud.ac.uk/news/2020/june/george-floyd-murder-and-the-history-of-racism/ (accessed August 2021).

House of Commons Education Committee (2021). *The forgotten: how white working-class pupils have been let down, and how to change it.* Available at: https://committees.parliament.uk/publications/6364/documents/69838/default/ (accessed August 2021).

Johnson A., M'gadzah, S.H., Watson, S. (awaiting publication) Autistic spectrum conditions in higher education during covid-19: Recommendations and support strategies. In: Meletiadou, E. (ed.) *Handbook of Research on Practices for Advancing Diversity and Inclusion in Higher Education.* IGI Global.

Katz, J. (2021) *Sarah Everard murder ignites a global conversation. Amanpour.* Available at: https://edition.cnn.com/videos/tv/2021/03/19/amanpour-sarah-everard-murder-protests-violence-against-women.cnn (accessed August 2021).

Iancu, I., Bodner, E., Joubran, S., Lupinsky, Y., Barenboim, D. (2015) Negative and positive automatic thoughts in social anxiety disorder. *Israel Journal of Psychiatry and Related Sciences* 52(2), 129–136. Available at: https://cdn.doctorsonly.co.il/2015/07/11_Negative-and-Positive.pdf (accessed August 2021).

John, T (2021) *Campaigners slam UK government report into racial disparities as a 'whitewash'.* Available at: https://edition.cnn.com/2021/03/31/uk/uk-racial-disparity-report-intl-gbr/index.html (accessed August 2021).

Kitto, E. (2020) *Tackle racism by teaching about our multiple identities.* Available at: https://www.tes.com/magazine/article/tackle-racism-teaching-about-our-multiple-identities (accessed August 2021).

Kline, N. (1999) *Time to Think: Listening to Ignite the Human Mind.* Octopus Publishing Group.

Kristof, N. (2016) *A history of white delusion.* Available at: https://www.nytimes.com/2016/07/14/opinion/a-history-of-white-delusion.html (accessed August 2021).

Lah, K. (2021) *All of this is part of daily life.* Available at: https://edition.cnn.com/videos/us/2021/03/19/kyung-lah-asian-american-experience-sot-vpx-nr.cnn (accessed August 2021).

Lewis, J. (2020) *Together, you can redeem the soul of our nation: Though I am gone, I urge you to answer the highest calling of your heart and stand up for what you truly believe.* Available at: https://www.nytimes.com/2020/07/30/opinion/john-lewis-civil-rights-america.html (accessed August 2021).

Lewis, D. (2021) *Race report: an exercise in delusion showing frightening detachment from reality.* Available at: https://www.mirror.co.uk/news/politics/race-report-exercise-delusion-showing-23830291 (accessed August 2021).

Lopez, H.I. (2021) *Dog Whistle Politics: Strategic Racism, Fake Populism, and the Dividing of America.* Oxford University Press.

Luther King M (1963) In: J. Lewis (2020) *Together, you can redeem the soul of our nation: though I am gone, I urge you to answer the highest calling of your heart and stand up for what you truly believe.* Available at: https://www.nytimes.com/2020/07/30/opinion/john-lewis-civil-rights-america.html (accessed August 2021).

Macdonald, K. (2021) Available at: https://www.bbc.co.uk/iplayer/episode/m000t96k/the-andrew-marr-show-14032021 (accessed August 2021).

McGhee, H. (2020) *Ted Talk: Racism has a cost for everyone.* Available at: https://www.ted.com/talks/heather_c_mcghee_racism_has_a_cost_for_everyone?language=en (accessed August 2021).

McGhee, H. (2021) *The Sum of Us: What Racism Costs Everyone and How We Can Prosper Together.* Random House Books.

McGhee, H. (2021) *Why racism hurts everyone regardless of race. Amanpour.* Available at: https://edition.cnn.com/videos/tv/2021/02/16/amanpour-heather-mcghee-racism-prosper-diversity-progress.cnn (accessed August 2021).

McKie, A. (2020) *How should universities approach decolonization?* Available at: https://www.timeshighereducation.com/features/how-should-universities-approach-decolonization (accessed August 2021).

McKinsey Global Institute (2021) T*he future of work after Covid-19.* Available at: https://www.mckinsey.com/featured-insights/future-of-work/the-future-of-work-after-covid-19 (accessed August 2021).

McLean, A. (2021) *Rescued from death row by a legal education. Alexander McLean and Jane Manyonge speak to Christiane Amanpour about the Justice Defenders, an organization providing inmates in Africa with legal training.* Available at: https://edition.cnn.com/videos/world/2021/03/12/intv-amanpour-justice-defenders.cnn (accessed August 2021).

M'gadzah S.H. (2017) Emotional intelligence: training of educational psychologists and applications in practice. Written evidence from Dr Shungu Hilda M'gadzah (CMH0094) original thesis 2011. In: *Government Green Paper. Children and Young People's Mental Health: Role of Education. House of Commons Education and Health Committees First Joint Report of the Education and Health Committees 2016–17.* Available at: https://www.publications.parliament.uk/pa/cm201617/cmselect/cmhealth/849/849.pdf (accessed August 2021).

M'gadzah S.H. (2020) First letter to white educational psychologists: We can't breathe – black Lives Matter. *Clinical Experimental Psychology* 6(3), 1. Available at: https://www.iomcworld.org/open-access/first-letter-to-white-educational-psychologists-we-cant-breathe-black-lives-matter.pdf (accessed August 2021).

M'gadzah S.H. (2020; unpublished) *Second letter to white educational psychologists: We can't breathe – black Lives Matter. What a difference a week makes ... or not, as the case may be. Complacency and complicity sit in the shadow of silence.*

M'gadzah, S.H. (2020) *Introducing a conceptual framework for understanding and dealing with racism.* Available at: https://www.linkedin.com/pulse/conceptual-framework-understanding-dealing-racism-m-gadzah/ (accessed August 2021).

M'gadzah, S.H. (2020) *Owning up to our negative automatic thoughts: diversity and inclusion in the boardroom.* Available at: https://www.inclusionpsychologists.com/post/owning-up-to-our-negative-automatic-thoughts-diversity-and-inclusion-in-the-boardroom (accessed August 2021).

M'gadzah, S.H. (2020) *We choose our politicians based on their identities and then adjust our interpretations of their policies to fit.* Available at: https://www.inclusion psychologists.com/post/we-choose-our-politicians-based-on-their-identities-and-then-adjust (accessed August 2021).

M'gadzah, S.H. (2021) *Building bridges of empathy and beyond unconscious bias. TNT 2.0 (Episode 64 with Dr. Shungu M'Gadzah - BUILDING BRIDGES OF EMPATHY by Teresa Quinlan).* Available at: *https://anchor.fm/teresa-quinlan/episodes/TNT-2-0-Episode-64-with-Dr--Shungu-MGadzah—BUILDING-BRIDGES-OF-EMPATHY-en2a31/a-a3cuh54*

M'gadzah, S.H. (2021) *On compassion, empathy and humanity: Black people are human beings and we are not animals.* Available at: https://www.inclusionpsychologists.com/post/on-compassion-empathy-and-humanity-black-people-are-human-beings-and-we-are-not-animals (accessed August 2021).

M'gadzah, S.H. (2021) *The prejudice–racism spectrum.* Available at: https://www.linkedin.com/posts/shunguhildamgadzah_racism-everydaychpsychology-diversityandinclusion-activity-6827654849891495936-271Z (accessed August 2021).

M'gadzah, S.H.(2021) *Check out this post by Sally Casterton.* Available at: https://www.linkedin.com/posts/shunguhildamgadzah_talkandvalue-psychvalue-talktodrshungum-activity-6823243708444528640-SHE6 (accessed August 2021).

M'gadzah, S.H., Doughty, D., Wardell, S. (2021) *Diversity and inclusion in the board-room (webinar).* Available at: https://youtu.be/3neAth8V9Og (accessed August 2021).

M'gadzah, S.H., Gibbs, S. (1999) Editorial: Challenging racism and inequality in education and child psychology. *Educational and Child Psychology* 16(3), 4–5. Available at: https://shop.bps.org.uk/educational-child-psychology-vol-16-no-3-1999-challenging-racism-and-inequality-in-education-and (accessed August 2021).

M'gadzah, S.H., Kamau, K. (2021) *What are your diversity, equity and inclusion resolutions for 2021? Available at https://www.inclusionpsychologists.com/post/what-are-your-equity*-diversity-inclusion-resolutions-for-2021 (accessed August 2021).

M'gadzah, S.H., Poate-Joyner, A. (2018) *Psychologists on boards: promoting greater inclusion.* Available at: https://www.inclusiveboards.co.uk/psychologists-on-boards-promoting-greater-inclusion (accessed August 2021).

M'gadzah, S.H., Saraon, S., Shah, T. (1999) Black consultants: a seminar on bilingual assessment, bridging the gap between the LEA and the community. *Education and Child Psychology Journal* 16(3), 68–89.

Minnesota Daily (2020) *Editorial: Can white people experience racism? Part II.* Available at: https://mndaily.com/233763/opinion/op-reverseracism2/ (accessed August 2021).

Mohdin, A. (2021) *Johnson's former race adviser accuses Tories of inflaming culture wars* Available at: https://www.theguardian.com/world/2021/jun/15/samuel-kasumu-boris-johnson-race-adviser-tories-culture-wars (accessed August 2021).

Moss, R. (2021) *How to handle disappointment: Be kind to yourself and the players. If you're feeling hurt today, just imagine the emotions the England squad must be facing.* Available at: https://www.huffingtonpost.co.uk/entry/how-to-cope-with-disappointment-after-englands-heartbreaking-euros-defeat_uk_60ebfe12e4b0cb62748426a5 (accessed August 2021).

Murphy, S., Walker, A. (2020) *MPs urged to do unconscious-bias training as dozens of Tories set to reject it.* Available at: https://www.theguardian.com/world/2020/sep/21/mps-urged-to-do-unconscious-bias-training-as-dozens-of-tories-set-to-reject-it (accessed August 2021).

Naftali, T. (2019) *Ronald Reagan's long-hidden racist conversation with Richard Nixon, 1971.* Available at: https://www.theatlantic.com/ideas/archive/2019/07/ronald-reagans-racist-conversation- richard-nixon/595102/ (accessed August 2021).

New York Times (2021) *How white Evangelical Christians fused with Trump extremism.* Available at: https://www.nytimes.com/2021/01/11/us/how-white-evangelical-christians-fused-with-trump-extremism.html (accessed August 2021).

Osaka, N. (2021). *Its OK to not be OK. Naomi Osaka on her first Olympics prioritising mental health and why sports needs to change – now.* Available at: https://twitter.com/TIME/status/14130989 44272474112 (accessed August 2021).

Prince Harry and Duchess of Sussex, Meghan (2021) *Oprah Winfrey interview.* Avail-able at: https://edition.cnn.com/2021/03/08/uk/meghan-harry-oprah-interview-recap-scli-gbr-intl/index.html (accessed August 2021).

Richard, L. (2021). *The Insider with Caroline Hill: Dr Larry Richard.* Available at: https://www.litera.com/litera-tv/episodes/ft-dr-larry-richard/ (accessed August 2021).

Roberts, G. (1992) The origins of delusions. *British Journal of Psychiatry* 161, 298–308. Cited in Gunn and Bortolotti (2008).

Russ, H. (2021) *McDonald's links executive bonuses to diversity.* Available at: https://stories.inclusify.io/media-story/mcdonalds-links-executive-bonuses-to-diversity/?fbclid=IwAR25JDjhGWrtqR8aaJzoRzwyPjcl4GLeLQmktwDAIQYfL9uKLVvbd-U_Tu (accessed August 2021).

Saadu, D. (2021) *How can we improve representation of black executives and non-executives in FTSE 100 companies? Recent research shows that black representation at board level is non-existent. Why is this happening in the UK? And how can organisations change their approach to turn the dial on racially diverse leadership?* Available at: https://www.hrzone.com/lead/change/how-can-we-improve-representation-of-black-executives-and-non-executives-in-ftse-100 (accessed August 2021).

Simonds, N. (2021) *Leadership lessons from chronic illness.* Available at: https://www.instagram.com/tv/CR9n7rypSaL/?utm_medium=copy_link (accessed August 2021).

Sinnott, J. (2021) *Football's coming home, but taking a knee divides England fans.* Available at: https://edition.cnn.com/2021/06/05/football/euro-2020-england-taking-a-knee-spt-intl/index.html (accessed August 2021).

Siregar, C. (2020) *Why do footballers kneel before a match? What 'taking the knee' means in sport.* Available at: https://www.goal.com/en-gb/news/why-do-footballers-kneel-before-a-match-what-taking-the-knee/10iqy03uyp5y01uh4x89dnaicz (accessed August 2021).

Stiffler, L. (2021) *The Black Boardroom Initiative launches with support from Seattle tech to boost board diversity.* Available at: https://www.geekwire.com/2021/black-boardroom-initiative-launches-support-seattle-tech-boost-board-diversity/ (accessed August 2021).

Syed, M. (2020) *Rebel Ideas: The Power of Diverse Thinking.* John Murray Press.

Todd, A.R., Bodenhausen, G.V., Richeson, J.A., Galinsky, A.D. (2011) Perspective-taking combats automatic expressions of racial bias. *Journal of Personality and Social Psychology* 100(6), 1027–1042. Available at: https://doi.org/10.1037/a0022308 (accessed August 2021).

Todd, S. (2021) *Is McKinsey wrong about the financial benefits of diversity?* Available at: https://qz.com/work/2038103/is-mckinsey-wrong-about-the-financial-benefits-of-diversity/?utm_source=email&utm_medium=quartz-at-work&utm_content=0d522257-f4a6-11eb-8191-2af58326e3c5&fbclid=IwAR32GgZn9eEvdMGVLw80gk8BW39GzKjnjIl5uUofknbjAionXgcaXjJKOMY (accessed August 2021).

Tuck, E., Wayne Young, K. (2012) Decolonization is not a metaphor. Decolonization: Indigeneity. *Education and Society* 1(1), 1–40. Available at: https://clas.osu.edu/sites/clas.osu.edu/files/Tuck%20and%20Yang%202012%20Decolonization%20is%20not%20a%20metaphor.pdf (accessed August 2021).

Turner, G. (2021) *A poem for humanity.* Available at: https://www.bizcatalyst360.com/a-poem-for-humanity/ (accessed August 2021).

Vedantam, S., Mesler, B. (2021) *Useful Delusions: The Power and Paradox of the Self-Deceiving Brain.* WW Norton & Company.

Walker, A. (1982) *The Colour Purple.* Harcourt Brace Jovanovich.

Wilber, K. (2005) *Introduction to Integral Theory and Practice IOS BASIC and the AQAL MAP.* Available at: https://integralwithoutborders.org/sites/default/files/resources/Ken%20Wilber_Introduction%20to%20Integral.pdf (accessed August 2021).

Wikipedia (2021) *Oprah with Meghan and Harry 2021.* Available at: https://en.wikipedia.org/wiki/Oprah_with_Meghan_and_Harry (accessed August 2021).

Wikipedia (2021) *Psychological manipulation.* Available at: https://en.wikipedia.org/wiki/Psychological_manipulation (accessed August 2021).

Wikipedia (2021) *The Colour Purple.* Available at: https://en.wikipedia.org/wiki/The_Color_Purple_(film) (accessed August 2021).

Williams, A., Weerasinghe, D., Hobbs, C. (2015) Guest editorial: race, culture and ethnicity in educational psychology. *Educational and Child Psychology* 32(2), 5–9.

Williams, M.T. (2020) *The intrusive, unwelcome thoughts of racism-themed OCD: OCD can cause people to live in constant fear of being a racist.* Available at: https://www.psychologytoday.com/gb/blog/culturally-speaking/202008/the-intrusive-unwelcome-thoughts-racism-themed-ocd (accessed August 2021).

Williams, T.A. (2021) *DOCTOR'S ORDERS The 4 ways to cope with England's heart-breaking Euros defeat.* Available at: https://www.thesun.co.uk/news/15569985/4-ways-cope-englands-heartbreaking-euros-defeat/ (accessed, August 2021).

Woodward, B. (2020) *Interview with President Donald Trump.* Available at: https://edition.cnn.com/videos/politics/2020/09/09/trump-audio-white-privilege-todd-dnt-tsr-vpx.cnn (accessed August 2021).

Woodward, B. (2020) *Rage.* Simon & Schuster.

Woodward, A., Mindock, C. (2020) *Taking a knee: Why are NFL players protesting and when did they start to kneel?* Available at: https://www.independent.co.uk/news/world/americas/us-politics/taking-knee-national-anthem-nfl-trump-why-meaning-origins-racism-us-colin-kaepernick-a8521741.html (accessed August 2021).

Useful links and resources

- **Allyship**
  https://www.linkedin.com/feed/hashtag/?keywords=allyship&highlightedUpdateUrns=urn%3Ali%3Aactivity%3A6783382853792092160

- **Association of Black Psychologists**
  https://ukabpsi.co.uk

- **Black Lives Matter**
  https://blacklivesmatter.com

- **Everyday Psychology**
  https://www.everydaypsychology.com/

- **Inclusion Psychologists Limited**
  https://www.inclusionpsychologists.com

- **Mentors in Violence Prevention (MPV)**
  https://www.mvpstrat.com

- **MIND charity**
  https://www.mind.org.uk
  https://twitter.com/MindCharity

- **Race Equality Matters**
  https://www.raceequalitymatters.com

- **Six Stages Framework website**
  https://www.sixstagesframework.com

- **Sussex Ehlers-Danlos Hypermobility Disorders**
  https://twitter.com/sedshsd

APPENDIX I:

The Six Stages diversity assessment and training courses

The Six Stages training programme helps people understand and challenge racism. It guides them as they identify any implicit or unconscious beliefs, values or behaviours they have or engage in, and ultimately allows them to reformulate their views and challenge their own prejudices. They will understand the ideas underpinning the framework and be provided with the necessary level of support as they pass through each of the six stages. Each stage is designed to support them while exploring their awareness and understanding of racism and how to respond to it. Participants are reassured by the fact that we are all at different stages of the journey towards creating a more equitable, non-discriminative society.

The Six Stages Framework is a dynamic and fluid developmental model – it is not linear. In other words, learning from each stage contributes to understanding and learning at the next stage of the person's journey. Individuals and their organisations can be at different stages in different areas of their functioning – thus the framework is more of a developmental matrix.

The bespoke racial equity and inclusion (DEI) training offered by Inclusion Psychologists Ltd relies on the carefully developed Six Stages conceptual framework. Our trainers ensure that the learning environment is safe and secure and that there is a no-blame climate. The sessions are ideal for teams because they provide an opportunity to share some of the challenges they face in a safe and secure group environment (see the *Testimonials and Feedback* section).

The diversity assessment

In exploring diversity and inclusion strategies, it is important to be able to identify some of the influencing factors such as the values, beliefs, attitudes and behaviours people hold or exhibit. Whilst appreciating that we are all at different stages in our journey towards understanding and dealing with racism and promoting an anti-racist agenda, the diversity assessments provide a baseline of where individuals and organisations are at the start of their journey.

The starting point is the 'diversity assessment', which is in the form of a questionnaire. It can also be used to review progress and measure outcomes. It can be completed with the support of a DEI consultant or psychologist. Follow-up assessments can be conducted as part of the progress-monitoring process to chart individuals' journeys and progress as they work through the framework. There are seven types of assessment, designed for use with different groups:

- individuals
- staff in organisations
- board members
- infants (ages 3–5)
- primary school pupils (aged 6–11)
- secondary school pupils (aged 11–18)
- university students.

For example, the diversity assessment for young people addresses the following:

- friendships and relationships
- understanding differences and racism
- dealing with racism
- being influenced by adults (teachers and parents)
- being influenced by peers
- identifying and experiencing racism.

Sample questions from the Individual Diversity Assessment

Racial and social injustice do not exist.
Strongly disagree | Disagree | Neutral | Agree | Strongly agree

I really don't see colour; I see everyone as the same.
Strongly disagree | Disagree | Neutral | Agree | Strongly agree

There are no such things as microaggression or unconscious bias.
Strongly disagree | Disagree | Neutral | Agree | Strongly agree

What about the working class? They suffer too – there is too much focus on race.
Strongly disagree | Disagree | Neutral | Agree | Strongly agree

I can recognise racist behaviour and language and I'm keen to correct this.
Strongly disagree | Disagree | Neutral | Agree | Strongly agree

Analysis of assessments

For each type of assessment, a supporting matrix is used to interpret the results. *Table 2* and *Table 3* provide examples of a matrix of developmental stages on the positive axis and an overview of the positive and negative axis, respectively, for understanding and dealing with racism for work with individuals. It is used to explore individuals' responses. Tables of conceptual frameworks also exist for use with boards, universities and schools.

The assessment relies upon triangulation of data from self-report measures, semi-structured interviews and a body of data collated by psychologists, DEI consultants and teachers. Inclusion Psychologists Ltd has designed a system that interprets the questionnaire results and provides the information as a visual display known as a radar report (Fig. 9), which assimilates the findings in a useful practical way, presenting information in several categories.

We supply our clients with their own radar report, a summary report and an action plan. More detailed reports are available on request, written by a psychologist or DEI consultant using the data from the Diversity Assessment and information derived from a specially conducted semistructured interview.

Note: The questionnaire may only be completed once as each applicant is given a unique ID number. There is a charge for each questionnaire, but licenses are available for groups.

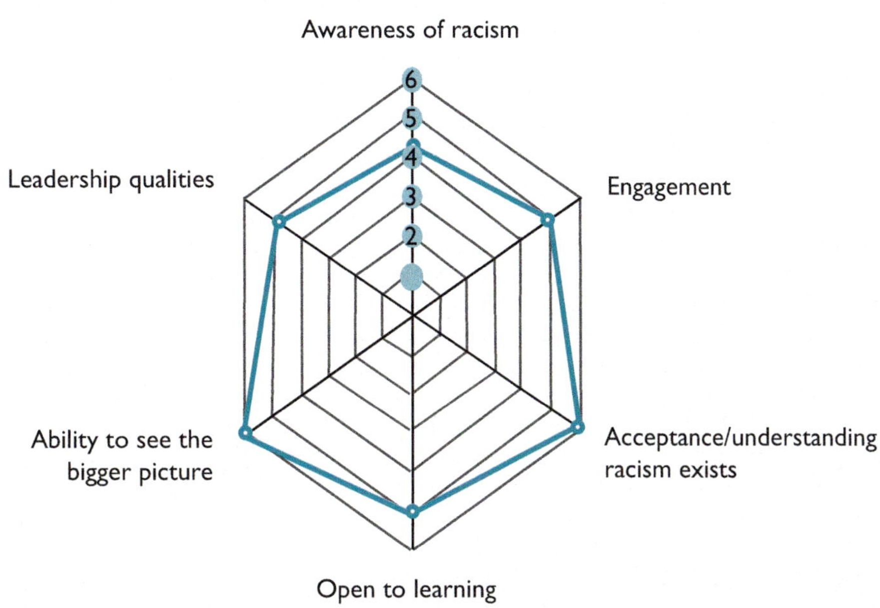

Fig. 9: Typical radar report – a visual display of the diversity assessment result.

Table 2: A matrix of developmental stages on the positive axis for

	Awareness of racism	Understanding of racism and engagement	Acceptance and understanding of the impact of racism
Stage +6 Leadership qualities	Aware of the need to address racism and racial injustice	Understands what individuals and organisations can do to dismantle racism	Recognises the impact of racism and social injustice on individuals Recognises the systems and structures that perpetuate racism
Stage +5 Ability to see the bigger picture	Is aware of the impact of racism and racial injustice	Has real understanding of what racism is and how it operates Understands institutional and structural racism	Recognises the impact of racism Recognises that racism is about power
Stage +4 Open to learning	Is aware of racial injustice	Accepts that racism exists Seeks to learn more about the experiences of BME groups	Begins to understand all forms of inequality including racism
Stage +3 Accepting that racism exists	Has increasing acceptance of anyone different Is aware that racism exists Quiet awakening to the existence of racism	Has increasing understanding of racism and racial injustice and how it operates	Accepts that there is such a thing as racism Becomes aware of biases, prejudice and discrimination and how this impacts on those who are different
Stage +2 Aware but dismissive and avoidant	Is aware of racial inequity and racism but dismissive of the issues	Has limited understanding of racism Is not interested in engaging in discussions	Feels sorry for past racial injustices – but is not really sure what can be done about them Focuses on gender equality and/or other issues – but not race
Stage +1 Unaware	Is unaware of and oblivious to issues of race Is ethnocentric Believes that black and ethnic minority people do okay Has no interest in racial injustice issues	Focuses on self and own ethnic group Is ethnocentric Has no interest in engaging with issues Has no interest in the experiences of black and ethnic minority people	Is not interested in issues of race or racial justice

understanding and dealing with racism (for work with individuals).

Beliefs and willingness to learn	Behaviours and ability to speak up and challenge inequality and racism	Leadership and shifting focus away from 'self'
Believes in humanity and everyone being equal Strives to understand 'self' and others from different groups	Speaks up when racism or microaggressions are witnessed	Supports others in challenging racism and all forms of inequality Takes on allyship roles Champions DEI issues
Strives to understand others from different groups Believes we are all 'humans first'	Often speaks up when racism and microaggressions are witnessed	Works with others to identify racial discrimination and inequity
Knows it is important to speak up when racism and microaggressions are witnessed	Sometimes speaks up when racism and microaggressions are witnessed	Is able to identify inequality and tries to point it out to others
Knows that racism is not a good thing and other black and minority ethnic groups can be negatively impacted	Stays silent and engages in bystander behaviours when racism or microaggressions are witnessed Downplays racism and tries to find reasons why it is not racism	Takes leadership roles in championing other equity issues Takes leadership roles in own ethnic group issues
Believes that other ethnic groups are not really their concern Stays and moves in own ethnic group or circle Ethnocentric focus	Speaks up and challenges when own group is being discriminated against	Rallies others to fight against issues of unfairness and inequality pertaining to own ethnic group
Believes each ethnic group is responsible for itself and focuses on itself	Recognises issues of unfairness and inequality relating to own ethnic group Is aware of other inequality issues such as gender and disability	Feels the need to do something to address inequality where it exists – but this does not include racial inequality

Table 3: Overall matrix presentation of a sample diversity profile to show how

STAGE –1	STAGE –2	STAGE –3	STAGE –4	STAGE –5	STAGE –6
Lack of awareness of racism	Dismissive of issues	Anger, attacking and rejecting	Anger/blaming of ethnic minorities	Extreme racial intolerance and racist views	Champion racist views
Unaware of issues of racial equity and racial diversity Unaware of relationship with issues of racial difference and racism Seem oblivious and ignorant to issues of race and suffering of those who are different Deny that racism exist No interest in talking about racism When issues of race and social injustice are raised, remain silent and keep heads down Uncomfortable when race and differences are mentioned Claim not to be racist or to 'see colour'	Aware of racial inequality, but dismissive of issues of race; racial injustice does not matter to them Avoid talking about racial inequalities and differences Believe the world is fairer than most black and ethnic minority people say Believe that racial and social injustice do not exist Claim not to 'see colour' Denial and discomfort when talking about racial differences resulting in avoidance, resistance and anger Prefer to talk about other inequalities e.g. gender, disability, the working class More concerned with issues such as abandoned puppies	Exhibit outrage and attacking behaviours Reject those who are different Resent the amount of time spent talking about racism Project own racism onto others Buy into stereotypes about those who are different Believe in conspiracy theories about racism Use racial stereotypes and accuse those who complain about racism of having a victim mindset Unable to show empathy or compassion to those who are different Believe that terms like 'micro-aggressions' and unconscious bias are unscientific or made up	Exhibit attacking and rejecting views of those who are different Extreme thinking and blaming of those who are different Believe those who are different are responsible for their plight and lack of success Use 'gaslighting' techniques to sow doubt and question beliefs Entrenched views and behaviours Become more extreme in their views At risk of being radicalised and groomed	Exhibit strong racist views and share them with others with a view to influence them Incite hatred and violence Can be verbally aggressive and threatening to those who are different At risk of extremism and violence Plot and plan to harm those who are different Understand systemic and institutional racism and issues of power	Able to take on leadership roles and negatively influence others Have extreme racist views and actively work to recruit others to their way of thinking Create false narratives and false world views that they sell to others Pose a threat in terms of radicalisation and grooming of others At risk of extremism, violence and terrorism

racism manifests on the negative and positive axis—characteristics and presentation.

STAGE +1	STAGE +2	STAGE +3	STAGE +4	STAGE +5	STAGE +6
Lack of awareness of racism	Aware of racism but dismissive and avoidant	Acceptance that racism exists	Open to learning	Able to see bigger picture	Leadership skills, promote racial equity and inclusion
Unaware of issues of racial equity and racial diversity Unaware of relationship with issues of racial difference and racism Seem oblivious and ignorant of issues of race and suffering of those who are different Deny racism exists No interest in talking about racism When issues of race and social injustice are raised, remain silent and keep heads down Uncomfortable when race and differences are mentioned Claim not to be racist or to 'see colour'	Aware of racial inequality and racism Dismissive of issues of race; racial injustice does not matter to them Avoid talking about racial inequalities and differences Believe the world is fairer than most black and ethnic minority people say Believe that racial and social injustice do not exist Claim not to 'see colour' Denial and discomfort when talking about racial differences, resulting in avoidance, resistance and anger Prefer to talk about other inequalities e.g. gender, disability, the working class More concerned with issues such as abandoned puppies	Increasingly aware of racism and racial injustice Recognise inequity and racism exist Express their discomfort and can feel overwhelmed Sense of helplessness and guilt Can still be unaware of own biases See themselves as advocates for those who are racially different Begin to discuss the issues with others	Open to learning and having meaningful conversations Open to new information, increasing understanding and knowledge Genuinely willing to listen and learn and to do the work and learning Able to challenge and correct their own and other's behaviour and language Can review and challenge own perceptions Show genuine compassion and empathy to those who are different Reflect and readily engage in conversations about racism and differences Freely share honest accounts of themselves as a white person	Start to see the bigger picture around race Able to reflect and genuinely engage in issues and discussions around race Able to explore and reflect on own biases and caves of privilege Understand systemic and institutional racism and issues of power Understand how structure and power effect individuals and organisations Recognise that injustice for one means injustice for all if unchallenged	Show leadership qualities and willingness to take on leadership roles to promote racial equity, inclusion and social justice Able to provide safe spaces for conversations on racism Understand the importance of values and values-based leadership Shift from just thinking about representation to considering values, beliefs and behaviours of individuals and organisations Actions are genuine rather than performative Speak up and challenge racism when they see it Show genuine allyship without focus on the self

APPENDIX II:

Courses and training for organisations and boards

The assessment and training programmes are aimed at chairs and board members in the private, public and voluntary sectors, including NHS trusts, social enterprises, local authorities, school and college governors, and charity trustees – any organisation that is looking to reflect on the impact of current issues on racial equity and wants to promote diversity and inclusion on their boards and throughout their organisations. We focus on using applied psychology and an understanding of behaviour and emotional intelligence (EQ) to achieve powerful outcomes for individuals, for their teams and for the organisation, especially when it involves diversity.

We provide psychologically safe spaces which enable us to work with you to explore uncomfortable and complex conversations. Our programmes and workshops enable individuals to explore different issues and how they respond to them. Feedback is provided to help them apply their learning and skills, both within the workplace and within the community.

DEI workshops and coaching with the Six Stages programme

- Training and coaching to develop racial fluency and racial literacy.
- Diversity assessments to identify understanding and how to deal with differences and racism.
- Support to promote inclusive cultures and inclusive leadership.
- Executive coaching for under-represented groups – women and black and ethnic minorities.
- Support to promote culturally intelligent systems and cultures.
- Support in developing allyships and networks.
- Training and coaching to promote emotional intelligence.

We provide psychologically safe spaces that enable us to work with you to explore uncomfortable and complex conversations. Our programmes and workshops enable individuals to explore different issues and the way in which your organisation responds to them. Feedback is provided to help you apply learning and skills, both within the workplace and within the community. These are the ways in which we can support you to grow and achieve change:

- Provide diversity assessments at individual and organisational levels.
- Provide reports and feedback proving insights and action plans for change.
- Apply intersectional cross-cultural lenses.
- Explore the key barriers to diversity and inclusion within the organisation.
- Increase understanding of the evidence base for promoting inclusive systems.
- Change programmes at different levels within organisations.
- Provide support to understand the key drivers for creating and sustaining inclusive cultures.
- Provide support to understand key concepts, such as privilege, and using this understanding to foster greater inclusivity.
- Draw on research and evidence-based understanding of ecosystems and organisations.
- Coach at different levels of the organisation with a focus on understanding of differences.
- Provide coaching and mentoring with a focus on strengths-based and resilience factors, as well as building confidence in women and black and brown employees.
- Embed D&I principles and frameworks at all levels within the organisation, including recruitment, onboarding, performance management systems and training.

Included in the training programmes

- DEI workshops exploring organisational culture and values-based leadership.
- Leadership training and coaching.
- Mentoring and leadership coaching for ethnic minority leaders – supporting them to achieve their goals.
- Diversity assessments and data analyses to help understand where the organisation is on its journey.

- Change programmes that foster diversity and inclusion, including talent development.
- Training for HR and people-development professionals.
- Onboarding, induction and supervision and appraisal programmes that are inclusive and strengths-based.
- DEI training for board members and Chairs of boards.
- Scripts and coaching for dealing with racial biases and differences.

Bespoke programmes designed to meet your needs

All programmes are tailored specifically for each organisation we deliver training to, according to its own priorities, and with the aim of embedding and underpinning its activities, goals and ethos. It can be considered as a golden thread running right through the organisation. It is effective in diverse organisational contexts, including:

- recruitment and retention
- interview panels and processes
- induction and on-boarding
- supervision (formal and informal)
- policies and impact assessments
- appraisals and 360-degree appraisal
- coaching and mentoring
- leadership training.

Training options

- Needs analysis – a consultation carried out by a DEI consultant from Inclusion Psychologists Ltd to understand your organisation and its needs.
- Initial consultation – discussion and analysis of individual or organisational needs.
- Standard training – a basic training programme introducing the Six Stages Framework.
- Standard training using the Six Stages conceptual framework – with group reflection and role-playing alongside support to think about how racism can be challenged.
- Group reflection – an opportunity for pairs and groups to reflect using case studies.
- Facilitator training.

To get the full benefit of the programme, we offer:

- full-day initial training sessions that aim to embed the framework into the organisation
- follow-up training days 4–6 months after the initial full day
- introductory 'taster' sessions based on the 'what' rather than the 'how'.

The prices of this training are available on request. Email contact@sixstagesframework.com or call (+44) 7956 965266.

Training for facilitators

Given the sensitive nature of this kind of training, it is important to create a safe space for challenging conversations to take place. There have been reports of businesses and local authority services who have carried out in-house Diversity, Equity and Inclusion training, after which some team members became upset. Discussing societal inequalities can be distressing for some people and it is important to safeguard against this. To this end, we train facilitators on how to create safe learning environments, following the principles of Nancy Kline's 'thinking environment' framework (Facilitation in a Thinking Environment, 1999), which helps foster a deeper understanding of the ways for dealing with challenging issues. It can be taught in a relatively short amount of time.

We also teach facilitators the skills required to support participants in the safe space (including listening skills, which are particularly important in the context of thinking about biases and prejudices) and what to do if a participant becomes upset during the discussions. We recommend group sizes of 6–10 for this type of training.

Prices of this training is available on request. Email contact@sixstagesframework.com or call (+44) 7956 965266.

Follow-up training

Follow-up training is highly recommended, especially for organisations in which there is a danger that Diversity, Equity and Inclusion matters will 'fall off the agenda'. Many local authorities and businesses have benefited from this already. These one-day sessions normally take place 3–4 months after the initial training. Booking a follow-up session allows organisations to review their progress and helps them focus on discussing and implementing individual and team action plans.

Note that Diversity Assessment questionnaires provided during follow-up sessions are subject to a discount. Participants must complete the assessments before attending the follow-up session.

The prices of this training are available on request. Email contact@sixstagesframework.com or call (+44) 7956 965266.

Measuring impact and outcomes

Inclusion Psychologists Ltd works with you to assess where you are as an organisation in relation to understanding and challenging racism. We measure this by establishing a baseline, then support you to set action plans and targets to move you and your team forward. One of my colleagues recently asked: *What tips can you offer for an organisation as part of their New Year's resolution initiative?*. I responded:

There are no shortcuts or quick fixes for DEI issues. These are the tips I would list:

- *Assess the organisation's starting point (baseline).*
- *Formulate a plan for what it wants to achieve and set timelines.*
- *Assess the employees' understanding of the issues and their ability to deal with them.*
- *Use a strategic framework, such as the Six Stages Framework, which is specifically designed to support organisations.*
- *Don't be afraid to ask for help – support may be needed to get started and to identify which cogs are stuck (and how to lubricate them!).*
- *Never 'volun-tell' black and minority ethnic or other minority groups to take part in DEI training because it can be overwhelming and have a negative impact on their mental health.*

Considering assessment or training or seeking further information?

For more information for individuals, organisations, boards, schools or universities, visit the Inclusion Psychologists' Six Stages Framework website (www.stagesframework.com) or register for an assessment here:

https://www.sixstagesframework.com/diversity-assessments/

You will then receive an email with a link to the Diversity Assessment questionnaire and a unique ID number.

Note that each questionnaire can only be completed once, and there is a charge for each Diversity Assessment questionnaire used. Licenses are available for groups.

APPENDIX III:

Testimonials and feedback on the training

A selection of comments from attendees of whole-day training programmes and those who have carried out the Diversity Assessments and received their report and action plan.

General comments

From Dr Helen Owen-Hughes, Educational Psychologist, Durham County Council

Having Dr M'gadzah work with our service was both a valuable and powerful experience. The full-day training on race, diversity and equality introduced us to helpful questioning tools and techniques, scripts and frameworks, many of which I continue to draw on both in both my professional and personal life. More than practical tools, though, the necessary confronting aspects of the training has left a lasting impression – the practice of looking inwards, exploring what forms our own identity, questioning and challenging our own prejudices and biases, perspective-taking, should be a core feature of every organisation (and individual!). I would encourage anyone who has the chance to listen to, or spend time with, Dr M'gadzah to do so!

From Mrs Joni Stidwell, Team Leader and Advisory Teacher for Equalities Education team

I attended a virtual professional development day led by Dr M'gadzah in September 2021. This session was aimed at Durham County Council staff working mainly within the SEND and Inclusion service, mainly consisting of Advisory Teachers and Educational Psychologists. Shungu's session was very powerful and thought-provoking. It encouraged each individual within the group to reflect on their own thoughts, feelings and perspectives as well as encouraging a unity within the group of how we can move society forward within our local area and through our own work. I particularly appreciated the six stages which gave some clarity to the direction and pathway we need to follow as individuals as well as a community. Shungu was able to use video clips and role-play to encourage active discussion and interaction throughout and the day whizzed by. As a member of staff who delivers training regularly myself, I can appreciate how challenging it is to try and initiate challenging thoughts, conversations and discussions and audience interaction through the medium of a screen, without the intimacy of face-to-face contact. Shungu managed to succeed and her session is something we have referred to and reflected upon within our team a number of times since.

Miscellaneous comments

Thank you so much Shungu and Shirley for two fabulous, enjoyable, challenging and energizing days.

Uncomfortable and challenging, but excellent!

I loved the training and the framework.

Terrific!

I have a framework to use when having conversations and will approach #drshunguconversationsonrace *in a different way.*

I can't stop thinking about yesterday's brilliant training session with Dr M'gadzah @Inclusionpsychs!

I haven't felt this excited or passionate about a piece of CPD for some time.

How useful did you find the training?

I found the training extremely useful because it added to my understanding of racism and improved my ability to deal with racism.

I think by the nature of the sessions, the first day provided more learning around understanding racism, whereas the follow-up training day was much more focused on supporting us to put our learning into practice.

Pauseful listening and SCARF model were very helpful in terms of offering an alternative/softer approach to 'challenging' and one that might be more fruitful.

I ended the day much more optimistic about us (self and team) actually doing something as a result of this training.

It was really helpful to see how Shungu helps people unpick things they say and experiences they mention, in a way that facilitates reflection rather than bring up defensiveness – thank you.

Discussing the history of racism and biases generally really helped with my understanding of racism.

One of the most interesting and useful courses I've attended in years!

Very useful – lots to think about and the Six Stages was a useful framework.

The experiential nature of the training lent itself very well to the subject and to enabling us to get the most out of the day and personalise the content.

Fantastic delivery – lots of discussion and food for thought.

It was also useful to have time to reflect on my own experiences and realise how much of my early life was spent in white-only environments, and what experiences since then have led to me being where I am today.

The 'caves of privilege' was a useful concept for me, alongside the Six Stages model of understanding and dealing with racism.

Also highlighted areas that I want to revisit (e.g. theories around group think; negative automatic thoughts), further reading (e.g. Noughts & Crosses) and further study (strength-based resilience).

Did the training add to how you might deal with racism?

The framework is extremely helpful and has helped me to reflect on how I have previously engaged in discussions around race, and things to consider for the future, not only on a professional level but on a personal level.

The pre-reading (history of racism) was especially helpful.

Discussions on stereotypes, biases and negative automatic thoughts were particularly helpful in exploring this further, as well as the pre-course reading. Also, the metaphor of the cave is a very helpful way of conceptualizing racism and prejudice and how/when people move deeper into their cave.

The Six Stages gives a very helpful framework and the role-play activity provided an alternative approach to my more usual response of direct challenge and confrontation, that I can see as being far more effective.

Small groups and then whole-group discussions were helpful, hearing others' suggestions, for example how to challenge stereotypes in a 'genuine spirit of psychological curiosity'. The key will be on how I implement this learning – and this is something that now depends on me, on my repeatedly doing it and learning from and reflecting on how I deal with racism each time I have to do this.

I think it definitely has but I will/would still be anxious about doing so.

I would like to know more about planning conversations.

Did the training meet your expectations?

Yes, I had hoped for a space for further reflection, to come away with an action plan (personal and team) for which I think we now have a good foundation, and to feel a little more empowered to take on the challenge of racial injustice, and feel I now have some tools that will help.

The follow up was described as invaluable in making some of our hopes and aspirations in the area of inclusion and diversity much more practical with a clear picture of how we will move forward as a team.

I was feeling somewhat discouraged concerning taking this forward as a team, as we seemed a few weeks ago to have lost our motivation, but today helped me to see that there is a level of commitment within the team to think about racism and what we can do to challenge racial injustice.

I think the day was perfectly pitched to support our goal of setting a clearer plan and way forward.

I was particularly expecting discussion around service delivery and how this links to racism and was pleased with the opportunity to explore this.

Definitely! It provided an opportunity to discuss a challenging subject as a group with honesty and openness.

Yes – one of my main expectations/hopes was that I would go away with something to do that I could review on day two, in a sort of action research way and this hope was fulfilled.

I also hoped that there would be a framework that would help us to consider racism and our response to racism as a team, which we were also able to do.

I wasn't expecting the training to be so reflective so yes, definitely.

It was no other training I've been on, I felt that you both (quickly) created a safe space to discuss some issues that we often shy away from. I also liked how you encouraged a group of educational psychologists to actively listen rather than ask clarifying questions etc. – powerful exercise.

It was more nuanced that I expected (in a good way).

I felt I had a voice to a greater extent that I expected (as a white person).

I possibly would have liked to understand/discuss the history of racism to a greater extent. The psychological concepts and models – added, precious stimuli and framework for thinking.

Role-play – useful to have something to apply the framework too and reflect on what was done and the impact of this.

I was particularly expecting discussion around service delivery and how this links to racism and was pleased with the opportunity to explore this.

What did you enjoy most about the day?

Shungu and Shirley's warmth as trainers; opportunities for reflection with others; being able to start creating an action plan and feeling positive and motivated to move things forward.

The participants reported that they enjoyed having the time and space to think about such an important issue as a team, facilitated by two wonderful and talented women.

Working together as a team on this matter; breaking frequently into small discussion groups with very defined tasks; facilitating everyone's voice being heard.

Seeing Shungu 'in action'!

Opportunity to be with colleagues; safe and facilitated forum to discuss racism; discussion around terms around race; the time spent reflecting on our own biases (and their impact).

Opportunities to reflect in small groups.

Role-play and discussion.

Opportunities to hear my colleagues' perspectives in this area.

Role-play between the presenters really helped my understanding of the framework.

Lots of practical tips and resources.

Discussions on stereotypes, biases and negative automatic thoughts were particularly helpful in exploring this further as well as the pre-course reading. Also, the metaphor of the cave is a very helpful way of conceptualizing racism and prejudice and how/when people move deeper into their cave.

The way you organized and planned the training to provide containment for a very emotive and difficult area so that it was a safe environment for talking, sharing, revealing, taking risks.

What did you find most difficult?

Identification of our own biases.

Knowing how to filter down what our priorities are/should be. Reflecting on own biases.

The use of terminology – what is appropriate.

Seeing and hearing some of the biases that I and others hold.

Being the only black woman in the room. I was very conscious of how others were responding to the training.

Knowing whether it would be ok to say some of the things I was thinking and/or to question some of the ideas being put forward.

The case study we didn't have time to do (though I am planning to suggest we do this in team meeting or perhaps another team forum) – I didn't know where to start on this.

Acknowledging my own biases. Identifying where these come from (still not sure about one of these).

Still not sure of the difference between unconscious and implicit bias (and if this difference is important).

What would you like future training to focus on?

I want to look at Nancy Kline's team meeting work. I'm going to regularly revisit the Six Stage model for understanding and responding to racism. I want to develop calm and respectful listening particularly when listening to people with different views.

Perhaps what we have 'done' in the in-between time – discuss why that is and what's next.

Having difficult conversations.

How to introduce training into schools.

Linked to both how to balance building bridges with not losing the focus on racism – can indirect approaches work? Are they acceptable?

Perhaps more around hosting helpful conversations.

About how you have used the framework in practice.

Further exploration of issues of racism and prejudice in our organisation and within our work.

Further ways that we can work with stakeholders around this issue.

Exploring and thinking about issues around segregation (e.g. segregation within some of our school populations).

Progress towards our personal action plans; next steps for our personal action plans; how we 'cascade' this training to others in the Authority; developing and implementing our service development plan in this area; how/if we take this out to our schools.

If this were face-to-face training I would include role-play, as I know that this is one of the ways I learn best (and I am aware that some people are wary of this way of learning).

What one thing might you do as a result of today's training?

Use the framework to adapt the way I engage in conversations around race.

The check-in and debrief offered by Shungu extremely helpful – I understand that this will be a standard offer moving forward.

A greater focus on terminology and checking this with people.

Read more about the history.

Challenge schools using the approaches shown by Shungu in the role-play.

Challenge stereotyping comments using the phrase, 'I'm genuinely curious about how you've reached this position' and other similar phrases.

Hear about how you have used the framework in practice.

Further exploration of issues of racism and prejudice in our organisation and within our work. Further ways that we can work with stakeholders around this issue.

Exploring and thinking about issues around segregation (e.g. segregation within some of our school populations).

Progress towards our personal action plans; next steps for our personal action plans; how we 'cascade' this training to others in the Authority; developing and implementing our service development plan in this area; how/if we take this out to our schools.

I would include more role-play, as I know that this is one of the ways I learn best (and I am aware that some people are wary of this way of learning).

What one thing might you do as a result of today's training?

Use the framework to adapt the way I engage in conversations around race.

The check-in and debrief offered by Shungu extremely helpful – I understand that this will be a standard offer moving forward.

A greater focus on terminology and checking this with people.

Read more about the history.

Challenge schools using the approaches shown by Shungu in the role-play.

Challenge stereotyping comments using the phrase, 'I'm genuinely curious about how you've reached this position' and other similar phrases.

About the Author

Dr Shungu M'gadzah is a psychologist and Diversity, Equity & Inclusion consultant at Inclusion Psychologists Ltd, and the creator of the Six Stages conceptual framework. She has senior-leadership and board-level experience in both the voluntary and public sectors. She was a senior leader in Local Authorities and Education at Head-of-Service level, where she led and managed multi-disciplinary teams. She has also worked in Higher Education teaching educational psychologists and has a doctorate in emotional intelligence.

Dr M'gadzah was the first black Chair of the British Psychological Society's Division of Educational and Child Psychologists (DECP) Committee (1999–2000).She also served on the British Psychological (BPS) Press Committee for four years and International School Psychology Association Leadership Committee. She was also previously Chair of the Association of black Psychologists in the UK and has been appointed onto several Boards to foster greater inclusivity and performance.

Find Dr M'gadzah online

Clubhouse

- Clubhouse club: Everyday Psychology. Name: Shungu. Handle: @drshungum.
- Clubhouse club: Six Stages Framework. Name: Shungu. Handle: @drshungum.

Facebook

- 6 Stages Diversity framework https://www.facebook.com/6StagesDiversityFramework/

- Dr Shungu Hilda M'gadzah
  https://www.facebook.com/hildashungu.mgadzah/
- Equality Diversity and Inclusion Psychology Network on Facebook
  https://www.facebook.com/groups/edipsychs
- Inclusion Psychologists
  https://www.facebook.com/inclusionpsychs/

Instagram

- Dr Shungu M
  https://www.instagram.com/dr_shungu_m/
- Inclusion Psychologists on Instagram
  https://www.instagram.com/inclusion_psychologists/
- Six Stages Framework
  https://www.instagram.com/six_stages_framework/

LinkedIn

- Diversity and Inclusion in Boardrooms
  https://www.linkedin.com/showcase/diversity-and-inclusion-in-the-boardroom/?viewAsMember=true/
- Dr Shungu Hilda M'gadzah
  https://www.linkedin.com/in/shunguhildamgadzah/
- Inclusion Psychologists Ltd
  https://www.linkedin.com/company/74196519/admin/
- Psychologists on Boards
  https://www.linkedin.com/groups/12182807/
- Psychologists on Equality and Diversity
  https://www.linkedin.com/groups/12368370/
- Six Stages Framework
  https://www.linkedin.com/company/74199229/admin/

Twitter

- Diversity and Inclusion in the Boardroom
  https://twitter.com/Board_Diversity/
- Dr Shungu M
  https://twitter.com/DrShunguM/
- Educational Psychologists on Race & Culture Forum
  https://twitter.com/EdPsyRCF/
- #edipsychs https://twitter.com/search?q=%23edipsychs&src=typed_query/

- Inclusion Psychologists
  https://twitter.com/Inclusionpsychs/
- Psychologists on Boards
  https://twitter.com/BoardPsychs
- Six Stages Framework
  https://twitter.com/6StagesFramewk/

Websites

- EVERYDAYCHPSYCHOLOGY
  https://drshungu.wixsite.com/website-9

Other media exposure

Essex Live: Koutsounia, A. and Lazell, L. (2021) Live Essex A-level Results Day 2021: Updates as students collect results across county after pandemic. Available at: https://www.essexlive.news/news/essex-news/live-essex-level-results-day-5764146 (accessed August 2021)

- *Glamour Magazine:* Spranklen, A. (2021) 'Have you got 'main character syndrome', the worrying Millennial condition when people view their life as a narcissistic film thanks to social media?' Available at: https://www.glamourmagazine.co.uk/article/what-is-main-character-syndrome (accessed August 2021).
- *Huffington Post:* Moss, R. (2021) How to handle disappointment: be kind to yourself and the players. If you're feeling hurt today, just imagine the emotions the England squad must be facing. Available at: https://www.huffingtonpost.co.uk/entry/how-to-cope-with-disappointment-after-englands-heartbreaking-euros-defeat_uk_60ebfe12e4b0cb62748426a5 (accessed August 2021)
- *Independent:* The physical and psychological benefits of being able to hug again could be huge. Available at: https://www.linkedin.com/posts/newspageuk_the-physical-and-psychological-benefits-of-activity-6795316149727842304-TnOD (accessed August 2021).
- *ITV Lunchtime News:* Discussion about mental health (5 May 2021).
- *Reading Berkshire News:* Leitelmayer, O. and Fowler, H. (2021). Berkshire students receive A-Level results from a year like no other. Available at: https://www.getreading.co.uk/news/reading-berkshire-news/live-updates-berkshire-students-receive-21270236 (accessed August 2021).
- *The Sun:* Williams, T.A. (2021) Doctor's orders—The 4 ways to cope with England's heart-breaking Euros defeat. Available at: https://www.thesun.co.uk/news/15569985/4-ways-cope-englands-heartbreaking-euros-defeat/ (accessed August 2021).

Index

C

D

H

I

J

K

L

M

N

O

S

T